SINGLE WOMAN
OF A CERTAIN AGE

SINGLE WOMAN
OF A CERTAIN AGE

29 Women Writers on the Unmarried Midlife—
Romantic Escapades, Heavy Petting, Empty Nests,
Shifting Shapes, and Serene Independence

Edited by **Jane Ganahl**

Inner Ocean Publishing, Inc.
Maui, Hawai'i • San Francisco, California

Inner Ocean Publishing, Inc.
P.O. Box 1239
Makawao, Maui, HI 96768-1239
www.innerocean.com

Cover design by Laura Beers
Book design by Madonna Gauding

Inner Ocean Publishing is a member of Green Press Initiative, a nonprofit program dedicated to supporting publishers in their efforts to reduce their use of fiber sourced from endangered forests.

We have printed this title on 50% postconsumer recycled paper with the recycled portion processed chlorine free. As a result, we have saved the following resources:

38 trees
1,793 lbs of solid waste
16,261 gallons of water
3,522 lbs of net greenhouse gases
6,540 kw hours of electricity

For more information, visit http://www.greenpressinitiative.org

PUBLISHER CATALOGING-IN-PUBLICATION DATA

Single woman of a certain age : 29 women writers on the unmarried midlife—romantic escapades, heavy petting, empty nests, shifting shapes—and serene independence / edited by Jane Ganahl. — Maui, Hawai'i : Inner Ocean, 2005.
p. ; cm.
ISBN: 1-930722-58-3
ISBN-13: 978-1-930722-58-3
1. Single women. 2. Middle aged women. 3. Self-actualization (Psychology) in middle age. 4. Autonomy (Psychology) 5. Middle aged women—Sexual behavior. 6. Quality of life. I. Ganahl, Jane.
HQ800.2 .S56 2005
306.81/53—dc22 0510

Printed in the United States of America

05 06 07 08 09 10 DATA 10 9 8 7 6 5 4 3 2 1

DISTRIBUTED BY PUBLISHER'S GROUP WEST
For information on promotions, bulk purchases, premiums, or educational use, please contact: 866.731.2216 or sales@innerocean.com.

contents

INTRODUCTION

Being an old maid is like death by drowning, a really delightful sensation after you cease to struggle.

—Edna Ferber, novelist

Spinster.

That's what we used to be called. If you were born with a vagina, remaining single "beyond the conventional age for marrying" (*American Heritage Dictionary*) was considered a fate worse than death. As recently as twenty years ago, single women of a certain age were viewed with a mix of pity and suspicion: if she has anything at all to offer, why doesn't she have a man?

To quote an ad that all the writers in this book would remember, we've come a long way, baby.

Single people in general are the fastest-rising demographic in the United States. A startling 26 percent of the population lives alone—that's quadrupled since 1940, when it was assumed that any right-minded gal would find a lad she liked well enough in high school, get hitched, and start making babies. And she would stay married no matter how unhappy she became.

These days, we're waiting until much later to marry, and if we divorce, we often don't marry again. Being married is no longer a presumption of adult life—and remaining single is now a conscious decision.

Surprising? Not really.

We unmarried women in our forties, fifties, and sixties have made our own lives. We don't need a man the way we used to—if we ever did. The marrying-for-kids issue is resolved as we either choose to remain childless or watch our little birds fly the nest. We have had a long career by this time—or even a second one. We have, with any luck, a strong network of friends to entertain us on dateless Saturday nights, friends to whom we can turn when we need support. We know how to travel alone. We are buying homes without partners in record numbers: last year, 21 percent of all real estate was bought by unmarried women, 10 percent by single men.

In other words, send us no flowers: we are not pining away.

What these record numbers also mean is that squadrons of single women of a certain age are on the prowl, looking for love— or at least a close approximation of it—if not marriage itself.

And dating looks a lot different at midlife than it does when you're young. Not better, not worse, just different. Sure, societal odds are stacked against a hot-and-heavy dating life once you've hit forty or so. We do live in a culture that worships youth. And where the mating game is always ripe for turbulence, women of a certain age find it even more complicated—thanks to the seesaw effects of aging. Our smarts are on the rise, even if our Hollywood-standard looks are on the decline. We become better at relationships, only to see relationship potential in fewer part- ners. As the laugh lines sprout and the gray hairs start to multiply too quickly to yank out, we're called upon to find new reasons to value ourselves—more reasons than we normally get from lovers.

But happily, our generation is rewriting the Book of Love as we go along.

Why not younger men? Why not recycle our exes? Why should a single mother not have an active love life? Why not go online?

Why not, indeed.

As this sociological phenomenon continues to play out in the media—which went into high gear with *Sex and the City*—we'll see all kinds of shows and stories about what unmarried women our age are really like. Are we stay-at-home old maids praying for a man to come along, as we used to be portrayed? Or are we more like Samantha from *Sex and the City*, with her hedonistic orgasm-fest of a life?

The truth, we all know, lies somewhere in between.

The truth is in these pages.

Inner Ocean's publisher, Karen Bouris, approached me after I wrote an essay for another of its anthologies, *Roar Softly and Carry a Great Lipstick*, on the self-esteem issues I was having as a single woman of fifty. She had also gone online and read several of the "Single Minded" columns I'd written for the *San Francisco Chronicle* since January 2002. (To everyone's surprise, including my own, my Sunday feature was a hit: proof that single people wanted to see their lifestyle reflected somewhere in the paper.)

Karen, smart cookie that she is, sensed an untapped market. She asked me to edit a new anthology of women writers—all unmarried, all over forty. "We'll call it *Single Woman of a Certain Age*," she said. I was sold. There was a need for these stories, and we would fill it.

Then began the rather delicate process of finding writers who were (a) terrifically talented and (b) not married. Several names you will read here are longtime acquaintances of mine, thanks to the annual Litquake literary festival I codirect in San Francisco every year; their marital status was known to me. But it was harder than I thought to ascertain the status of others I had my eye on.

"Hello! I'm a big fan of your writing! . . . And can you please tell me if you're hitched?"

I would eventually make allowances for two women who are living with a partner—Merrill Markoe and Kim Addonizio—because I was intrigued by their perspectives on what it takes for happily single midlife women to agree to cohabitate again.

But other than the requirements of (ahem) ripe age and unmarried status, I left the assignment wide open: tell me a story about being single at midlife. Sure, it can be about love and romance (and there is much of that herein), but it can also be about the other, more ephemeral, elements of our lives. Body image, the joys and sorrows of solitude, the freedom to test ourselves, balancing motherhood, petting in all its forms.

I flung my net wide when looking for writers and came up with a multinational, multiculti cast of characters. Australia is represented twice, India once. Writers hail from New York to Seattle, L.A. to Montana. And, of course, several from my native Bay Area. We represent a cross-section of ages, from barely forty to the luminous Jane Juska at seventy-two. Most of us hover between forty-five and fifty-five.

The lineup set, essays started to come in, and with each new arrival I gasped with delight. These are women who have been around the block—many times—and it shows in each wise word. With age, the saying goes, comes perspective. Even as these intimate tales will make you laugh—and possibly cry—there is much to be learned here.

Reading these pieces, I recalled Gail Sheehy's take on the years between forty-five and sixty-five. The author of the best-selling *Passages* books calls midlife "the age of mastery"—a time to decide who we really are, to jettison our false selves, and to figure out how we want to live the rest of our lives.

"Ah, mastery. . . ," she writes. "What a profoundly satisfying feeling when one finally gets on top of a new set of skills . . . and then sees the light under the new door those skills can open, even as another door is closing."

Clearly, the twenty-nine women in this anthology see doors opening all around them, even as they grapple with some that are closing.

Section 1—"The Dating Game Has New Rules"—is all about opening new doors. Five essays contain five different perspectives on the vagaries of dating at midlife. If one has been out of the game when divorce or the death of a spouse comes, it can be pretty scary to consider flirting, dating, or, worse, having physical contact.

As Irene Sherlock notes in "Singles Dance," "the last man I had an in-depth conversation with was that car mechanic, and it was about carburetors." This explains the presence of Pepto-Bismol as she prepares for a girls' night out.

As Ronnie Caplane, whose husband died two years ago, writes in "A Date": "It's been thirty years since I sat across a dinner table from someone whose underwear I didn't buy, and I don't know the rules anymore."

Joyce Maynard decides she'll give online hookups a whirl, only to find herself with a coffee date who seems incapable of speaking without using song lyrics. She writes: "If Bob Dylan or Neil Young or Jefferson Airplane—or even Donovan—hadn't said it first, the experience did not exist."

Ellie Slott Fisher is open about her misadventures as a single mother trying to get her love life back online. She vows to keep her sex life private from her children. "A cool mom is one thing," she notes, "but a red-hot mama is utterly disturbing."

And finally, Dakota Cassidy, married for many years and divorced around the age of forty, decides to try online dating and is deluged with eight hundred responses. "I'm a frickin' Victoria's Secret supermodel!" she crows.

If the women in section 1 are test-driving the new dating game, the writers in section 2—"Prince Charming = Santa Claus"—are challenging it. These are women who have been single most of their lives, women who are a bit disenchanted with the fantasy aspect of romance and dating. At the same time, they still risk, they still love—and sometimes they still hurt.

Merrill Markoe, after saying she would "Never Again" move in with someone, finds love is much more . . . interesting in her forties: "A little like tiptoeing barefoot over a frozen pond, into a dense, dark forest, hoping to make it to the cozy cabin without being buried in an avalanche or unexpectedly tumbling into a snowy ravine."

Debra Ginsberg challenges her man's thinking about marriage—and her own—as they take a "Detour" on a long drive. In "Remember Me?" Liz Byrski lays bare the hard-learned lessons of trusting someone when trust is not warranted; and Laura Fraser confronts a two-timing former lover—and her own conceptions about what she wants from a man—in "My Last Two-Night Stand."

And the inimitable Ms. Gonick, thinking she was done with romance as she becomes her parents' caretaker, meets Mack, a cowboy who makes her "Beaks Benedict" for breakfast. Hay bales have never seemed so sexy.

In section 3, "Stretching toward Bliss," writers tackle a host of challenges that many middle-aged women can identify with—often in creative ways.

April Sinclair sends us her essay "Straight outta Marin," in which she finds herself in a "modern-day Mayberry"—and up against stereotypes about single middle-aged African American women. Kim Addonizio ponders how it is that she is able to live with a man, love him, and still fall in love with others—like her harmonica teacher and all his "Blue Notes." Wendy Merrill considers plastic surgery as an option as she confronts the dual challenges of menopause and addictions—to both alcohol and men who keep her "Falling into Manholes."

Sunny Singh, who has never wanted to marry or settle down, finds herself challenged by falling in love in "Fear of Meeting Mr. Right." Judy Blunt takes her eighteen-year-old son to a birthday skydive in "Airborne"—and wonders if fear will change them both. And Spike Gillespie, tired of a lifetime of nowhere relationships, tries something new with a much-younger soul mate: love without romance. They are "Nothing like Harold and Maude."

Section 4—"Going It Alone"—delves into a topic that every unmarried woman must confront. Solitude can be blissful liberation—or it can be lonely. And no matter who the woman is or what she's made of, a solitary life takes some getting used to.

Lynn Freed opts to move to the country, which is cause for celebration until a rapist starts prowling her town and she finds herself "Locked In." In "One Single Day," Kathi Kamen Goldmark installs her son at school, comes home to a divorce-empty house—and exults in her first book signing as a new novelist.

Isadora Alman finds that two friends who once had so much in common now have "Two Lives" that could not be more different. Anne Buelteman chooses the sometimes lonely life of a stage gypsy in "The Glamorous Life"—but the tradeoffs are excellent.

Jane Juska chides a woman friend for not "Cutting Loose" her fears of being alone: "We're so intent on ending up not alone we miss out on what can come before the end and sometimes, in our desperation, we drown the possibilities of life." And Sam Horn similarly celebrates her boys' leaving home and the joys of "The Open Nest."

Finally, as section 5—"Other Kinds of Love"—illustrates, there are more kinds of love than the not-always-satisfying romantic love. Unmarried women know this truth well. Our passions are boundless—stronger at this age than ever—and encompass our kids (or our nephews and nieces), our pets, our world (oh, the beauty of travel!), and, most especially, ourselves.

Susan Griffin finds "A Secret Joy" in losing herself in the tiny towns of Provence and in the lives of strangers she meets: "the particular rapture that belongs only to solitude."

Rachel Toor and Patti Lawson have both found excellent

stand-ins for the affection of men: four-legged beasts. In Rachel's case, she does her "Heavy Petting" with a virtual menagerie of critters; Patti finds respite from loneliness in the exuberance of one homeless dog who gives her "A New Leash on Life."

Susan Maushart is barely able to worry about her own hormonal meltdowns; her daughters are right there with her in the "House of Hormones." And Diane Mapes finds that playing the role of "Charlie's Aunt" to a darling nephew is more than enough to satisfy her need to parent.

Finally, Cameron Tuttle takes a break from her too-fast life for a little self-examination—in front of the mirror—in "Nude Awakening." "Swaying to a sultry Aaliyah tune, I gaze upon my full-length, naked body. Wow. There is more of me than I remember."

I won't spoil it by telling you how it all turns out.

Oh, and one more thing. It turns out that *spinster* also means "someone who spins." These twenty-eight other writers have some whopper tales to spin. I hope they inspire you as they did me.

—Jane Ganahl

1.

THE DATING GAME HAS NEW RULES

And What about Getting Naked?

You will do foolish things,
but do them with enthusiasm.
—Collette

The absolute yearning of one human body for another
particular body and its indifference to substitutes is
one of life's major mysteries.
—Iris Murdoch

SINGLES DANCE

Irene Sherlock

Lately, I've been dogged by a chronic nauseated feeling. Not unlike morning sickness, it hits hardest at certain times. I step into the shower and see myself slamming against the tile, felled by a bar of soap on the floor. It doesn't actually happen—I just get an image, and my stomach lurches.

Or like tonight. I'm getting ready to go to my first "over thirty-five" singles dance, and I'm sure the elastic will break on my skirt when I'm standing in the middle of the dance floor.

I don't have anything against dances per se. I just never thought I'd be at one ever again. But I've been mulling over the whole idea of men these last few weeks, and as a potential interest in my life they do appeal. Before this, I never truly considered how I would find one once I was ready. My friends, I thought, would have an adequate supply of single men they would rustle up, or there would be someone at work or . . . somewhere. Just about half the population is male. How hard can it be to get a date?

Hard. My stomach is rumbling now in a sick, nonhungry way. Most of my friends are married and so are their friends. They shrug and remind me that single men my age can and do date much younger women. Up till now, I have relied on the pool of men who might actually want to date women their own age. I believed it would be a fairly deep pool, considering my minimum requirements—some education, a sense of humor. This brings me to the requirements that men have, which in turn brings me over to the mirror, which in turn reminds me of the frail elastic in my skirt that is planning to break.

And to this churning in the pit of my stomach. The fact is, I am not ready for this dating thing. Not ready for the singles life. Malcolm was right, telling me I was more in love with the safety of marriage than I was with him. If I head into that man-woman bingo game out there, won't that be acknowledging to the world I don't have that safety net anymore? I snap the elastic on the skirt as a test and then go into the kitchen for some steadying chardonnay.

"I'm sorry, so sorry," Patsy Cline is singing behind Rebekah's closed door. My daughter has eclectic taste in music. She likes Hendrix or Madonna, depending on her mood; on really iffy days she likes Patsy Cline. Last night, she argued with her boyfriend, so today, Patsy sings the country blues. This evening I can relate to her, a woman who knew how to ache about life.

Back in my room, I apply Trésor perfume to parts of my body that for a long time haven't been touched in the way I would like them to be. It seems absurd to be applying perfume to a body that is about to go to a Unitarian Fellowship dance. I do it anyway, ignoring my anxious stomach.

The one small catch is that I don't dance. Can't dance. I used to dance a million years ago at the Good Shepherd Friday-night dances, where Mary Pat and I would do the hully gully, or a reasonable facsimile thereof, but you lose something when you graduate from high school, and for me it was the confidence to dance. Since then, I have felt foolish and naked whenever I try to move my body to music. Unlike other people bumping and grinding up on the dance floor, I am painfully aware that I have no rhythm. I have little coordination and an obstinately inhibited part of my personality that I haven't dealt with, therapy notwithstanding. Twice I've sprained my ankle in aerobics class simply trying to follow the instructor. It's hard for me to watch and do at the same time. I would make a terrible voyeur. Then again, it's hard not to watch other people while you're dancing. They're so much better than you are. Or they care so much less. So, because of this dancing thing, singles dances have not been an option.

Until now.

I move into the bathroom and carry my chardonnay along. Rebekah has set my hair in hot rollers and is standing ready to activate her army of brushes and combs to give me what she calls a "calculated messy look." I wonder what kind of man this will attract.

"Sit," she orders, and then turns my chair away from the mirror. "I don't want you looking at yourself."

I steal a glance anyway. I look like one of those saleswomen in the perfume section of Lord & Taylor. "You need eyeliner," she says, going through my makeup bag. I stand and down the last of my wine. Enough, I tell her. That is not me in the mirror. If I meet a guy tonight, and if I ever see him again, he'll never recognize me.

My daughter eyes my long black skirt. Her own skirt must be all of six inches long, showing her fleshy thighs. "How can you dance in that thing?" she asks. I do not have the heart to tell her that I don't plan on dancing, that my fondest hope for the evening is to meet someone with whom I might have a civil conversation. We'll move off to a room where you can talk and have some coffee, me and this nondancing, hunky Unitarian who will get my juices flowing.

Rebekah is part of the reason I am going out. She has watched me stay home most weekends while my soon-to-be ex-husband has been out wining and dining a series of women (this is on Rebekah's authority). She is worried that she will move out, get married, and visit, years later, to find me still sitting in my living room with only Meals on Wheels as company.

She launches into an earnest speech about how she thinks—no, she knows—I am going to meet someone tonight, someone who likes dogs and who is there not because he's a Unitarian—whatever that is—but because he knows I am going to be there. Me.

How sweet. I smile at her. Her arms wave an arc of hair spray over my "do." She is right, I tell myself. I look great, if not like myself. I certainly smell great. "You may be right," I tell her. "I may get lucky tonight."

"You go, girl." She snaps the cap back on the hair spray.

In the car, my confidence founders, and I have to give myself another talking to. *I'm beautiful, and I'm available.* Also, I remind myself that I shouldn't judge a book by its cover. So what if he seems shy and dweeby; I'm not exactly the picture of confidence. And I need the practice. The last man I had an in-depth conversation with was that car mechanic, and it was about carburetors. Be sociable. Ask questions. *Be available.*

Mount Kisco is a half-hour drive, and that gives me time to play my favorite tapes and drink Pepto-Bismol. The rain has let up. My stomach is starting to feel better. I might actually have a good time. There's a beautiful full moon tonight, and Sheryl Crow is plaintively singing, "Are you strong enough to be my man?" Sing it, Sheryl.

Ten minutes into the ride, I have to pee, so I pull over on a dirt road and turn off the lights. I find a discreet spot in the bushes. Suddenly, there are headlights in the distance. I crouch down and pee faster. The car turns down another road. When I stand, I realize I have peed the entire length of my skirt. The two napkins I find in the glove compartment do not help. So much for my lavishly perfumed body. I wonder what kind of man this will attract?

Connie is waiting at the door when I arrive. She's wearing red lipstick and a shortish black skirt. Connie is a veteran of the singles scene but has been lying low for a while. It gets depressing, she says, seeing the same faces, week after week, at different places along the circuit. If singles dances are such a great way to meet people, why aren't these people meeting someone and staying home? I reasoned that some of them must have met someone. Though not fully convinced of this, Connie has agreed to be my tour guide for the evening.

At one time, Connie knew every singles dance spot within a fifty-mile radius: where the country music crowd hung out, which places were upscale or divey, where you might find a slightly older, professorial type or a hard-dancing, truck-driving kind of man. She had her own radar, she said; she could spot a married man fifty yards away. Connie knew about cover fees, drink prices, where the best buffets were, and how much they cost. She also knew where the quiet jazz clubs were, where you could just sit and have a drink and maybe get looked at, if that's all you wanted.

But Connie wants more than that when she goes out. She loves to dance—and to loud rock and roll. This Unitarian dance is a departure for her. She heard about it from someone at work, and since she had recently quit smoking, and since most singles places were a smoker's paradise, she said we could check out this non-smoking, wine-and-cheese thing, although she couldn't really vouch for anything that was sponsored by a church. Sounded kind of tame, she said. Fine with me, I said. I liked tame. Tame was my middle name, and I prayed for a coffee room. Or a comfortable ladies' room I could hole up in till she was done. Oh, why didn't I bring a book?

"I hope they play some decent music," Connie says as we go through the large wooden doors. The building is modern, like a school, not a church. Two women at a card table take our money and write our names on name tags. Loud music blasts from the darkened auditorium. I hear a DJ calling—"Ladies' choice. It's ladies' choice." I look around for anything resembling a coffee room. We pass men and women, all with name tags, milling about. The place is packed and there is no place to hang our coats. We throw them over a pile in the back, then head for the ladies' room. Connie wants to check her lipstick. I need to pee again. Just like high school, I think. Some things never change.

In the restroom, we meet a woman in a floral chiffon dress who looks to be in her sixties. She's a regular at these things. "You're gonna have a ball!" she says, a bit too enthusiastically. I catch a glimpse of myself in the mirror. The chardonnay has worn off and my upper lip is sweating. God knows what my underarms are doing. And then there is the issue of my still-damp skirt.

I look at my hair. It has lost its calculation and now just looks messy. Connie asks if I want hair spray. I feel sick again, duck into a stall, and finish the last of my Pepto-Bismol. When I come back out, she is reapplying her lipstick. I watch her and clutch my purse to my chest. OK, I tell myself. I can still make a run for it.

"Ready?" Connie asks brightly. We head out the door.

We make our way to the auditorium, where men and women are crammed onto a packed dance floor. Others are standing around in groups of twos and threes. Everyone seems to know each other, talking and laughing, as we elbow our way through. The dance floor is lined with tables and chairs, all taken. Barry Manilow is singing about the Copacabana—a song I haven't heard in its entirety in twenty years. I think of my brothers playing in their rock band ages ago, making fun of Barry Manilow. How my mother said at least that was music.

Insanely loud music at that—and most of these people are older than we are. Also, two-thirds of them are women. Connie is pissed, I can tell. Pissed because she likes men her own age or younger, pissed because she senses this place is going to be a dud.

I only know I have a headache because I haven't eaten since

lunch. We cannot get near the wine-and-cheese table, and when we do, we find picked-over cubes of Swiss cheese and a couple of warm carafes of chablis. We hold our plastic cups in our hands and look around the room, at the others around us who are talking and dancing. A couple who look about eighty glide by. Two women with terrific tans start a line dance in the middle of the floor. Pretty soon there is a whole crowd line dancing to Barry Manilow. Connie is muttering in my ear about killing the person who recommended this dance. We are definitely the youngest people in the room. It is then that I wonder what I am doing here, when I could be home taking a perfectly good bath. Home—where there are food and clean clothes and something to read and no Barry Manilow.

Connie looks over at me. I try to smile, but this is no time for pretense. She mutters something. "What?" I screech over the music. This is a bad dream. I am in one of Dante's circles of hell, and I will wake up any moment in my bed, which means I will not have to drive home or ever think about this place again.

We find two empty chairs and sit, thank God, because by now I feel as if someone were standing on my chest. A silver-haired man passes by and smiles sweetly at us. Two women in short cocktail dresses come over to tell us we are sitting in their seats. We stand. The music begins again. This time, a rumba. We watch the couples on the dance floor. Some of these people can really dance. Some of them are as bad as I would be if I were out there with them.

"They may be old, but some of them can move!" Connie nudges me, swaying her hips. I realize she wants to dance, even here. I also know I will never do this again—try to meet men at a dance. High school was bad enough.

The music shifts to a cha-cha, and my head begins to pound. A serious-looking man with black glasses appears by my side and asks if I want to dance. Actually, I do know how to cha-cha, one of the few dances I can do, however badly. "Go on," Connie says, nudging me toward the dance floor. The man takes my hand. His fingers are clammy.

"So," he says, moving on the dance floor. "Come here often?"

I smile. "First time."

"I'm Peter," he shouts over the music.

"Irene!"

Peter looks to be about fifty-five, and he's a pretty good dancer. He snaps his fingers to the music. "So, Irene, where are you from?"

One, two, cha-cha-cha. "Connecticut!" We are literally yelling at one another.

Peter slips his arm around my waist. It's a confident gesture, and my body stiffens automatically.

"You know," I say, pulling away. "I'm sorry. I don't feel well."

"Oh," Peter says. He knows there are plenty more fish in this Unitarian sea. "Be well, Irene." I watch him move through the crowd. Then I go and stand beside Connie, who sighs, first at me, then at the place in general.

"Ten dollars," she says. "What a rip-off." We get our coats and leave.

We find a pizza place that is loud and full of drunks. I don't care. I'm just so glad to finally breathe again. I order a beer and listen while Connie fills me in on the real places to go, places where there are much younger men. She tells me about Teddy's and its Sunday-night singles dance, where for the same ten dollars we just squandered, we could have gotten a fabulous all-you-can-eat buffet. I think she wants to head right over there. I eat my pizza in silence. I cannot wait to get home.

In the car, I pull down the rearview mirror and stare at myself. For the first time since Malcolm left, I take a hard look.

Here I am—alone at forty-eight, and maybe I'll stay that way. I don't have the character or the skill or the perseverance to find and fall in love with someone. Why didn't I just stay married? *So what if we didn't like each other?* People don't have to like each other—only to endure.

By the time I pull into the driveway, I've stopped crying. I pray that Rebekah is sleeping; I cannot bear to face her questions tonight.

Instead, I find her in the bathroom, kneeling in front of the toilet, vomiting. I crouch down beside her and take off my coat. She was at the movies when it hit her, she said. Finally, she has caught the flu bug or whatever it was that her boyfriend had the previous week. Her head over the bowl, she gags before heaving. When she looks up at me, her voice is ten again. This is the same young woman who created my wanton-vixen hairdo. "Do something," she implores. "Can't you give me some kind of medicine?"

I walk her to bed, then retrieve a large bowl from the kitchen. I find ginger ale and a cool washcloth for her forehead, but nothing seems to help. For another hour, I watch as she continues to get sick. It is then that I realize we are both stricken with a "bug": hers is viral; mine, more nebulous. Still, they will both reside within us, these foreign bodies, wreaking havoc within our systems for days or weeks or longer. And there is nothing either one of us can do about it except to live through it.

CHaI with WOODSTOCK

Joyce Maynard

Fifteen years divorced and pushing fifty with a short stick (to borrow a phrase from an old boyfriend of mine, though back when he and I knew each other, the landmark age that short stick was poking was forty), I decided to give online dating a try. Never the type to hang out at bars, and—being a self-employed writer—recognizing that whole days go by (weeks, sometimes) when I hardly leave my house, I thought the Internet was a sensible and efficient way to put myself out there, as it were. And to see who might be out there, putting himself out, in a similar fashion.

So I gave myself a moniker—Red Shoes—and signed up on Jdate.com, a site for Jewish singles. The cost was $39.95 a month—cheaper if you choose the six-month option, but (being the optimist I was) I chose to believe I might not need six months to find myself a true and loving partner. One I might actually love back.

More often than not, the monikers people choose for their online dating lives are likely to offer up a clue about the person—more than one might suppose, though it is generally only after you've invested a little time in them that you understand the significance and—retroactively—realize the red flag was out there waving in the breeze the whole time.

This particular individual (dating prospect number 473) called himself Woodstock, and from his age (fifty-six) I figured out he'd probably been there. He was one of those people who evidently believe that the plural of a word requires the use of an apostrophe, a trait I've always found disturbing, but I was trying to look on the positive side. Woodstock looked to be in good shape, though not (like a few of the men on display) so ostentatiously as to feature a photograph of himself shirtless. He had never been married (always a little suspect in a man that age; one feels strangely more comfortable with an indication of at least one divorce), but he did say he'd had a number of long-term relationships, and that his former partners were all still friends who would happily offer recommendations if called upon. So far, so good.

He worked as a freelance sound man, but really, he was a musician—guitar player. The ability to play a stringed instrument remains a longtime weakness of mine, and because it does, I knew it meant his finances would be tight, if not downright nonexistent. This has never been a deal breaker for me, however. And there he was, smiling out at me with a faintly otherworldly look—wearing a beret over longish and graying hair pulled back in a ponytail, quoting one of my all-time favorite Leonard Cohen songs, "I'm Your Man." How could I not write to him?

He was online at that very moment, so within minutes, he was writing back. This time with a line from Neil Young: "I'm just passing through on this old freight train." In the letter I sent back, I asked him a few of the basics—where he lived, whether he'd come from California originally or moved here more recently, like me. It was Jerry who'd brought him to the Bay Area, he wrote back. This I understood to mean Garcia. As in the Grateful Dead.

As for where he lived . . . this was a little vague. There was a reference in his note to house-sitting (translation: not a homeowner). He liked to spend time in Mendocino, Grass Valley, Berkeley . . . but for the moment at least, he was crashing (a word I hadn't heard since the 70s, probably) with this buddy in Sausalito, ten minutes from me. For the time it took to e-mail, he wrote, we could be chilling over a cup of chai down the hill, what did I say?

I should have been working, but the morning had already gotten away from me (had turned into the afternoon, in fact), and I was no doubt looking for a reason to do something other than work. So I said sure. I ran a comb through my hair, checked myself in the mirror, and decided I looked as good as I was going to that day.

Twenty minutes later, my Toyota was pulling up in front of Peet's, and I was surveying the faces for one that matched Woodstock, whose real name, I now knew, was Keith. And though the demographic of men who might be found in early afternoon having coffee or chai outside Peet's strongly favored the very age group of Woodstock/Keith, it wasn't hard to locate him. (Though as I did, I realized that the photograph he'd posted to accompany his profile had probably been taken a few years back. The hair— though just as gray and still pulled into a ponytail—was considerably sparser. The African cap was the same.)

"You've been a long time coming and a long time gone," he said when he spotted me—and rose from the table to reveal a dashiki-style shirt and a pair of bell-bottoms. It took me a minute to place where I'd heard this before. Crosby, Stills, and Nash.

"I'll just get my coffee," I told him. "Do you have yours yet?"

"Could you get me a chai latte? Grande."

Not that I should have been noting these things, perhaps, but those run $3.75. "I meant to stop at the ATM first," he said, making a gesture in the direction of his pockets, without actually pulling any money out. He gave me a smile that had probably charmed women back around 1970.

I came back with our drinks. "You know what Jimi always said," he told me.

Jimmy? I was basing my references in the regular world. Of people I actually knew, as opposed to people whose records I owned, or once did. Probably on vinyl. As I realized when he added, "Hendrix."

"Castles made of sand fall in the sea eventually," he said. If there was a context for this, it escaped me.

"You knew Jimi Hendrix?" I asked him. Hopelessly literal, that's me.

"Knew him, man? Let's just say, he knew me. Knew my blood, man. Knew my fucking shit. Knew every fucking thought and feeling any lousy human being had on the fucking planet. The man knew God. Let's just say, the man *knew*."

"I guess music is important to you, huh?" I said. Truthfully, it had always been to me, too, but I didn't share his impulse to go around quoting song lyrics.

"What else is there, man?" he said. "And you and me . . . we lived through the great days. Jimi. Janis. Jerry. They knew where it was at."

I might have pointed out that they had all died of overdoses, too, but that seemed unnecessarily obvious.

"So you work in the music business?" I asked him.

"All my life. Roadie with the Mamas and the Papas. Came this close to making it with Michelle Phillips one time, back in '68. Joni Mitchell gave me a pack of gum, backstage, at Monterey. Joni was something, man. She knew. . ."

". . . where it was at?" I offered.

Exactly. How did I guess?

"*There* was a babe," he told me. "You know the song where she mentions the man doing the goat dance? That was me."

"So what have you been doing lately, Keith?" I asked him. "In the last thirty years, I mean."

"Time, time, time," he said. "Time is an illusion . . ." This was clearly a song, but not one I was familiar with.

Something in all of this—maybe the knowledge that we hadn't even gotten to the death of John Lennon yet and I was already feeling depressed—was making me feel desperate to change the course of the conversation. "You have any kids?" I asked.

He gave me another of his boyish grins, though this time, when he did, I could detect severe dental problems. "Never felt that urge to be a breeder," he said. "Not that kids aren't mind-blowingly cool. I'm just more a kid myself. Came out here in '69, looking for Jerry, and I haven't stopped grooving since."

I had taken only two sips of my chai at this point, and already the cup was looking bottomless. All I wanted was to have it empty. To get out of there. But of course it wouldn't be enough to finish my drink. There was his chai to be gotten through as well, and from the looks of things, he took his slow.

"It takes a lot to laugh, it takes a train to cry," he said. "Dylan. The poet master. The fucking poet master."

"Keith," I said. "I have a feeling this isn't going to work out. I'm not really your type." I might have added, *"Good-bye is too good a word, babe, so let's just say fare thee well,"* but I didn't want my knowledge of song lyrics to get him started again.

"Hey, man, we were just getting started," he said. "I was just thinking to myself how you were even cuter than your picture." These were the first words out of his mouth that appeared not to have been thought up by someone else, and in other circumstances they might have been flattering ones, too. Still, it wasn't enough to keep me in my seat. I had already decided, screw the chai. Just get out of here.

"I'm sure you've got a lot to offer, Keith," I told him. "But I just don't see the two of us together."

No point explaining. The same thing that had, so fleetingly, seemed charming online—namely, this man's ability to summon the lyrics of certain songs I also liked—was not simply a way of embellishing his own thoughts and feelings, drawing comparisons where they applied. The lines of songs—from the looks of it, exclusively songs written more than three decades ago—were all he had in his vocabulary. The only way he had of expressing emotions, the only language available to him. If Bob Dylan or Neil Young or Jefferson Airplane—or even Donovan—hadn't said it first, the experience did not exist. The man did not possess a language or vocabulary of his own. Never mind the other part—that in the ten minutes that constituted the sum total of our relationship, for all eternity, the man had not asked me one question about myself.

"I don't want to hurt your feelings," I told him. "You seem like a great guy. . ."

"Hey," he told me. "It's like Jerry said."

In spite of myself, I had the feeling—knowing that he was now dipping deep into the pool of so many liner notes' worth of accumulated poetry and pseudopoetry—that Keith might actually be on the verge of offering up something at least moderately profound to sum up the end to our astonishingly short-lived relationship. "Remind me," I said. "What did Jerry say?"

"Keep on truckin'," said Keith. He was up from the table before me, even. He took his chai with him.

unmarried . . . with children

Ellie Slott Fisher

Four of us, all single moms, were sewing costumes for our children's fourth-grade play and nibbling peanut butter brownies that I had nervously made from scratch when our lighthearted conversation turned from school gossip to dating horror stories. "Did your kids ever catch you and a date in a compromising position?" I asked.

"What? Are you kidding? Of course not."

Was it just me? Could I be the only irresponsible single mom who had gotten caught? Maybe it was the liberation that comes with being over forty or the comfort of being with kindred souls, but I confessed. Late one night I'd let my boyfriend slip in the back door while my kids slept soundly in their beds. I ran downstairs to answer his knock, dressed in an emerald silk spaghetti-strap number—my well-worn "I Love Mom" nightshirt kicked in a ball under my bed. As I became wrapped up in his embrace, losing all sense of my physical surroundings, I barely noticed the tiny voice from above.

"Mom?" My brain began to defog. "What are you doing downstairs?

"Oh, you mean *that* kind of compromising position." One after another, my single-mom companions suddenly recalled their own close encounters—the guy hidden in the bedroom closet, the boxers left on the bathroom floor. I was not alone in my irresponsibility, and in fact, I was in the majority among dating single moms. There are a lot of us, by the way. Some thirty million moms live alone with their children, and two-thirds of those women have children over eighteen.

Dating at any age is not without challenges. But dating as a middle-aged woman with children living at home is a little like downing a pint of Ben and Jerry's Chunky Monkey. It feels wonderful when it's just the two of you, but the minute you come to your senses, you feel guilty as hell.

When divorce or death unexpectedly sends us back into dating, the issues we face as mothers require extra sensitivity, intelligence, and awareness. Ha, easy for me to say. I suppressed all of those critical traits the first time I set out to date as a single mom. Since I had been happily married for a long time, the prospect of dating had gone the way of discos and ironed hair (mercifully), replaced with the comfort of being in a permanent committed relationship. Then my husband of fifteen years passed away of an undiagnosed genetic heart arrhythmia. I was thirty-eight, and our children were young, my daughter nine and son five. At the time I couldn't conceive of myself with another man, though I also couldn't imagine my children growing up without a dad.

A little over a year after my husband's death, I was asked out by a friend of a friend whom I had met briefly at a bat mitzvah. When I broke the news to my kids that I was going on a date, my son was ambivalent, being more interested in whether the cool babysitter was coming—the one who let him overdose on sugar and stay up until the noisy garage door heralded my return. My daughter, on the other hand, old enough to appreciate the possible evolution of Mom's dating, wanted no part of meeting my date and asked to stay overnight at a friend's.

Having experienced dating as a teenager with my parents waiting up for me—rather than my kids—I had no point of reference as to how to handle this development with my children. So I tended to be less than candid about details of my dating, careless about the unexpected passion, and ignorant of my children's own unique sense of timing. When I met a divorced father through a personals ad, I lied to my kids, telling them that he was a fix-up, and shocked them when, after two months, I declared I was getting married.

So much for my once-considerable sensitivity, intelligence, and awareness. Despite never wanting to hurt or worry my children, I failed to appreciate their perspective or give them time to acclimate to my dating, much less my remarrying. After nearly three years and the realization I had made a mistake, I divorced him. The next time I entered the dating world, I was determined not to repeat my errors.

This time I approached my social life differently. I was honest with my kids from the outset. I told them when I had a date and with whom, not a significant amount of detail but the important data—what his profession was, where he lived, whether he had kids, and what their ages were if he had them.

I also understood that my children required significant time to process my dating. My feelings toward a man—whether positive or negative—grew fairly quickly. But what might have seemed to me to be a long-term relationship felt to my kids like a couple of brief encounters. Now, before I even told them I was going away with a man for a weekend, I let them know I liked him well enough to date only him. That's a necessary and gentle precursor to breaking the news to your kids that you're thinking of getting married. I'm not sure what I had been thinking my first time around. My kids had met the cat groomer more times than my second husband, and I had never considered making *him* a permanent part of our life. In retrospect, maybe I should have.

And then there's the passion. Yes, passion did set in unexpectedly when I resumed dating after a lengthy marriage. I didn't recognize myself when I transformed into a sexually confident woman. The mere idea of being intimate with a man other than the one who had benefited from my best physical years had been enough to frighten me at first into never dating. Like most other middle-aged women, I had become so comfortable hiding my expanding middle or new crop of cellulite that I dreaded looking in the mirror, to say nothing of having sex with the lights on. But I was pleasantly surprised to find a renewed interest in sex. It came back to me easily, a little like riding a bike. Only this time it was without the training wheels.

Painfully aware this second time of the need to refrain from passionate moments in the proximity of my children, I became more conscious of my timing. Kids have a way of waking up or coming home from school at the most inopportune times. I knew that my children wanted no part in the intimacy of my dating. They didn't want to see the lingerie I purchased for the occasion, or overhear my dusky conversations on the phone. While I promised my children honesty, the boundary was drawn when it involved sex. A cool mom is one thing, but a red-hot mama is utterly disturbing.

Still, my dating has taken a huge burden off my kids as they have gotten older and entered college. My having a strong adult relationship with a man—in the absence of their dad—has taught them how to have similarly healthy adult relationships. And although I value committed relationships with men, my children also know that they are, and always will be, the most important people in my life.

Dating is simply one item on a long list of challenges faced by single moms. Compared with the afternoon fifteen years ago when my daughter broke out with chicken pox moments before the doorbell announced her twelve girlfriends, sleeping bags in tow, and a clown costing $125 an hour, dating as a middle-aged single mom has been a piece of cake.

Then again, it's taken me years to perfect my peanut butter brownies.

A Date

Ronnie Caplane

Date *n.* *6a.* an appointment for a set time, esp. one for a social engagement with a person of the opposite sex. *vi.* *2.* to have social engagements with persons of the opposite sex.

—Webster's New World Dictionary

"I have a date," I say, bursting into Frankie's office. "It's not really a date date. It's a getting-to-know-you lunch date, but it's with a man and he's single and available and straight."

He got my name from mutual friends. Our five-minute phone conversation was easy and playful, and I was excited. After my husband died, I didn't think I could ever be excited about another man. Sure, I wanted another husband, but I didn't want to date to get one. Within forty-eight hours of getting the terrible news that Joe's helicopter had crashed, I began thinking about whom I might get for the job of husband, but that had nothing to do with excitement and everything to do with practicality. My personal dam had ruptured, and I needed someone, anyone, to shove into the opening to stave off the flood. It wouldn't be another Joe, there couldn't be another Joe, but I just needed a stand-in, someone whose life I could jump into while mine was being patched and shorn. No getting-to-know-you, no dating, just a man who was willing to step into the role of husband and would spare me the pain, the loss, and the changes that I knew were inevitable. With a new husband, I could carry on as if nothing had happened. It turns out that I was not the first widow to think along those lines. Fortunately, I didn't act on it. Unfortunately, many do.

But now I am almost two years out and ready to take the baby steps that finding a new partner, or even fling material, requires. But it's been thirty years since I sat across a dinner table from someone whose underwear I didn't buy, and I don't know the rules anymore. This is scary stuff.

"I need your help," I tell Frankie.

A year earlier, when I first arrived at the office, a shell-shocked widow, Frankie offered to be my dating counselor. I didn't think that day would ever come, but Frankie knew better. "When the time comes, I will be your coach," he said. With three marriages punctuated by two rounds of desperate middle-aged dating, Frankie qualifies as an expert. Not only does he have the requisite experience, but by his own boastful admission, he has made "every mistake in the book."

"What should I wear?" I ask.

"Lose the boots," he says, giving me the once-over.

"I can't wear boots?" I say. All I have is boots. "I'm not investing in new shoes until I know whether this is going somewhere."

"Boots are OK, just not the dominatrix ones," he says, indicating my pointy-toed, spike-heeled, calf-high black leather boots with the silver buckle on top. "They'll scare him."

I don't even know how tall this guy is. What if he's short? Joe was six-two. I could wear anything with him. But maybe I can't wear any heels with this guy. I don't want to tower over him. What if he's insecure? I haven't worried about this stuff since adolescence, when no male was as tall as I was. There were years of slouching and keeping my knees bent. I had a whole arsenal of tricks to disguise my five-foot seven-inch frame. I can't go back there. I won't go back there.

"Where are you going to eat?" Frankie asks.

"I don't know. We haven't decided," I say. His office is on the other side of town. When I told him mine was in the Civic Center, he called it "geographically undesirable." I'm not sure what he meant by that, whether it was about snobbery or inconvenience. Inconvenience I can understand, but snobbery I can't abide. Maybe I should have asked him. We have great ethnic restaurants—they're just dives. Maybe I should offer to go to where he is and avoid the whole thing. If lunch is too complicated, maybe he'll change his mind and decide it's not worth it. Muni's easy. I could do that or grab a cab. He's got better restaurants anyway. I wonder if that would be OK.

"Will I look overeager if I offer to go to where he is for lunch?" I ask Frankie.

"Yes," he says firmly. "First date, he comes to you. Go to Hayes Street Grill. It's perfect, upscale but not excessive." Before I can ask, he answers my next question. "And let him pay. We can discuss financial arrangements later."

For the next three days I experiment with different outfits, polling the men in my office as to what they like best. I keep track, eliminating various component parts.

I have no idea what this guy looks like. I don't even know what I want him to look like, so I study strange men to see who appeals to me. There's the guy at the gym with the beard and the biceps, and the tall studious one in the elevator with the dark hair and hint of gray at the temples. Either of them would do just fine.

Then reality hits. I'm looking at men I would have gone out with when I last dated. This fellow isn't going to be thirtysomething. He's going to be . . . middle-aged. I Google him. From what I can put together, he's in his mid-sixties, maybe older. If he has any hair at all, it's gray and thinning, and he probably isn't going to be fit and firm. He could have a paunch.

I stop looking at men.

"He hasn't called, and we never decided where to meet," I say, throwing myself down on a chair in Frankie's office. It's Thursday morning, and I'm worried that my lunch date forgot about me or changed his mind or lost my phone number. "I hate this." I haven't started dating yet, and already I'm anxious. "Can I call him? He gave me his phone number. Maybe I'm supposed to call him."

"Give him until four this afternoon and then we'll talk," Frankie says. "Maybe he's away on business. If you liked him from that phone call, then he probably likes you. Maybe he doesn't want to seem too eager. I went out with this woman I really liked. The next morning I showed up at her office with a gift. That scared her away. She never took another call from me again."

"But what about reservations? What if he doesn't call until tomorrow morning?" I say. Friday lunch at Hayes Street is busy. "I'll never get reservations that late."

"Make reservations now, but don't tell him," Frankie advises. "Make him think you're important enough to get in at the last minute."

He calls that afternoon. Yes, he will come to my end of town. The restaurant I name is fine. He'll check in tomorrow morning to finalize everything.

"How will I recognize you?" I ask when he calls the next morning.

"I'm wearing a brown sweater, and my hair's a little too long," he says.

"You have hair," I say. "That's great."

At noon, Frankie and a few of the other men in the office gather to see me off. I'm wearing a knee-length black skirt, black patterned tights, black nondominatrix boots, and a chartreuse sweater. I adjust my sweater, and they give me a thumbs-up. "You got money just in case?" one of the men asks. Another tells me to call the office if anything goes wrong. I realize that I finally have the big brothers I've wanted all my life. I thank them, give them the most confident smile I can, and walk to the door. I brace myself as I open the door, remind myself to breathe, and take the first step into this new life that I never wanted.

FROM WIFE to PROM QUEEN in the CLICK of a MOUSE

Dakota Cassidy

Yep, I'm single.

Single and hovering near forty.

With two sons and two dogs, a cat, and my mother.

Sweet, huh?

Lemme tell ya, it ain't nothin' like *Sex and the City*. Not even a little.

Their clothes are *way* better.

So are their bodies.

Sigh.

I didn't plan on being single. I was married for nineteen years, and it just happened. Just like that. Well, OK, that's not exactly true . . . He was unfaithful a number of times. I was blinded—a number of times. Then God gave me the gift of blessed sight.

Like in a real 20-20 kinda way.

It was a long battle, but I got the booty and that was kind of nice. I went through hell and back, two thousand miles of distance between us to get it, but I'm peachy now.

That brings me to the single part of this.

OK, so I'm single, I'm reasonably healthy and all-right-looking, and I know I'm totally ready to date. I do have a small factor that weighs heavily in my negative account. I work at home. It's not as though my fellow authors and I get together and go out after work, ya know? That means no happy hour at five sharp in my neck of the woods. It's a bitch to meet guys at happy hour when happy hour is at my house and said happy hour is an hour in the day you're actually feeling happy and that happy feeling has absolutely *nothing* to do with being in a bar, after work, a little margarita chugalug and some cute stud calling you "baby" as he moves closer to your bar stool. My fellow authors are my colleagues *and* gal pals. They live all over the world. We can't even have girls' night out. It's damn hard to coordinate a girls' night out when one of your best buddies lives in Zimbabwe. Essentially, this means, as a writer, working from home gives me little opportunity to meet anyone other than the UPS man, who isn't really that cute. I don't have anyone to go out dancing with, so I can't scope out men in, like, a bar. I ain't goin' alone, that's for sure. You absolutely must have a friend to go to a bar with. It's like a girl rule or something.

But I digress.

So I get this brainstorm. I'll join an online dating site. Yeah, I'll join an online site, reputable, mind you, that will give me scores of men to choose from like a Saturday-night police lineup. It's easy. I can do it from my office chair, and, most importantly, I can be selective about whom I go out with.

So I scour the Internet. There are more date sites than Viagra ads. I'm astounded. Who knew? So as I check each site for its requirements, I also check for the kinds of things they ask you to fill out. Height, weight, hair color, sexual-position preference.

OK, so that isn't the site for me.

As I narrow my search, I decide to skip the sites that ask you what *type* of relationship you're seeking—a serious relationship, a friend, or a fuck buddy.

Animal, vegetable, mineral.

I'm in this to find someone who wants to pursue the joys of *fidelity*, exclusivity, loyalty. I want to skip through the fields of green with my soul mate—or at the very least a really cool guy who wants to boink just *me*.

We don't have to book the Four Seasons for the buffet banquet, because really, who wants to be divorced again, but I wouldn't mind a boyfriend. Ya know, hand holding, a smooch every now and again, dinner, even a shared granola bar if push comes to shove.

OK, so I find the right site. It has an instant messenger so you can chat, and it gives you a fairly in-depth look at the profiles of all the yummylicious men. It even provides the distance you'll have to travel if you find you want to hook up—*and* an e-mail account.

Well, I did pay for a gold membership . . .

Cool indeed.

I write up a snappy profile (I am a writer), and I include all of the nifty stuff about me, me, me! I'm even honest enough to list my true weight and say my body type is average. It really is, I swear.

Yeah . . .

Anyway, I give all of my requirements for my soon-to-be stud muffin. I slap my picture up and walk away a winner. I fully expect to get like ten e-mails in the course of my three-month gold membership.

As a matter of fact, I'm damn well counting on it.

I go off to bed and think happy date thoughts. Of course, keep in mind, I married at eighteen. My last date was McDonald's, pre–Happy Meals, and a basketball game.

Whatever.

I arise bright and early the next day to find that I've received notification from the site that I have mail!

Yippee skippee! I feel pretty. . .

I grab some coffee and a smoke, and I settle into my office chair. I log on to the site, and everything just explodes. I mean, like, my in-box—literally.

I am the proud recipient of eight hundred e-mails.

Yes, you read that correctly.

I am overwhelmed. I am astounded.

Holy shit, I'm a frickin' Victoria's Secret supermodel!

I am speechless, a rare occurrence for me, but nonetheless an event I can assure you some would love to witness.

I push my jaw shut and gaze, alternating between stupid and blank, at the computer screen. And so my journey begins. . .

I begin sifting through this e-mail, one "Hey, sexy lips" message at a time. The locales are peculiar to me. I did specify my *home* state as a requirement, didn't I? I check my profile. Why, yes, yes I did.

So who in Bangladesh wants to date little old me? That's another thing. It seems my eyes in my profile's picture speak to everyone from here to said destination of Bangladesh.

I feel like a prom queen, captain of the cheerleading squad, and Shania Twain all rolled into one.

Then I realize that men are simple creatures sometimes (relax, not always), and they know not what they do. Surely they couldn't have known what they were doing when they e-mailed a woman who specifically said she wouldn't date a serial killer, right?

Two hundred discarded whack jobs, an offer of a palace, a herd of sheep, marriage proposals, poems, romantic scenarios where I end up naked on the couch, monetary gifts, abuse of the King's English, and a partridge in a pear tree later—I have some serious contenders.

Oh, except the guys who think my lips are *purdy.*

Yes, purdy. It would seem my lips speak to men, too. They talk just like Angelina Jolie's. My lips have been called many names in many e-mails. Not a single mention of my nose. . .

All right, so as I adjust to my hottie, gorgeous, angelic, goddess, most-beautiful-woman-alive status, I weed out some more nuts. Now, I write humor for a living, so not toying with some of these men and their e-mail is like asking me to attempt writing *War and Peace.*

I just can't, so I don't.

I am compelled to e-mail the man who says he doesn't want to sound goofy, but my lips look juicy. I ask him in my reply, what about that doesn't sound goofy to you?

I respond in kind to the man who asks if I have arms and legs by divulging that, no, I don't. I'm just one big head. My body is of great interest to about 20 percent of the men who e-mail me. I used only a head shot in my profile, and yes, it really was taken *this century,* I swear.

I ask the man who writes me a romantic scenario where I'm naked and waiting by the door with a beer whether he minds if I invite my neighbor over for a ménage.

I ask the nice twenty-four-year-old surfer dude who's hangin' ten if he minds that I hang ten, too—in more places than not, on my body.

Then I giggle maniacally because I'm just cracking myself up.

Then I get serious about the men whose intent seems genuine. Sorta.

I peruse their profiles diligently, as if I'm qualified to sniff out the bipolar schizophrenics. No offense to them, but I have my own issues. Surely as a couple, it could get downright ugly, ya know?

Ahh, now I make a selection or two, and I e-mail them back. Actually I e-mail almost *everyone* back. I decide to cut the serious contenders some slack, figuring that leaving their gray matter intact is essential to a good first date.

I've narrowed the field, and now I begin to spend some time getting to know a couple or twelve of them via e-mail. We banter, we make light, we tease, we even flirt.

I'm having a great time because words are my strong suit, my arrows, my cyber feminine wile. As we get to know each other, they ask *what* I write.

Sigh . . . OK, so I have to be honest, and I'm not ashamed at all about the erotic content in my books. The only difference between my books and what we writers call a mainstream romance is, the bedroom door is wide open.

Hell, I take the hinges off!

I wallow in my carnality every single day. I'm not having sex, so in my mind someone should be, and I want a piece of it. So I write it. It's the vicarious thing.

Very safe, totally consensual, and admittedly voyeuristic to a degree.

Whatever.

So the ever-touchy question is, should I tell or shouldn't I? Either they're going to freak out, or they're going to read me a verse from the Bible, or they're gonna wanna do me on date one. It's a crapshoot.

I'm going to give the men who contacted me huge kudos here—not one of them reads me a verse from the Bible. One guy is a little jiggy, though. He says I am so beautiful, why didn't I become a secretary? Um, that job was taken?

OK, so let me dispense with the getting-to-know-you phase of this. Suffice it to say, we got to know each other, and I was finally comfortable enough to go on my first date in twenty-one years. The men I chose to date weren't necessarily hunk-o-licious. They were a combination of attractive and intelligent—in e-mail, anyway.

I agree to meet one date, whom I'll call Fill-in-the-blank, in a well-lit, safe public place.

I pack a bag of handy datelike items.

Mace, a Louisville slugger, stuff that every date-savvy girl should have.

I share with my sons that Mom has officially begun to scam the boy-toy market and they're just going to have to deal with it. Oh, and I tell my mother too, because she's the babysitter, ya know?

Actually, I don't explain it like that at all, but that discussion is better left for an epic saga on *Dr. Phil*.

I'm not in the least nervous as I prepare. I slap on some makeup and some cute jeans, and out the door I go with a wiggle of my fingers over my shoulder.

Ta-ta for now and all.

I meet my date at a local bar for a drink. I'm not much of a lush, but a drink or two and I'm all good. A drink or seven and my date is not. As I enter the bar, I am pleased to see that my date looks just like his picture. He, too, is pleased to see that I look just like mine. He reminds me, on drink four, that he's had an experience or two with women who post pictures that are from their heyday. I forget to mention that the pom-poms should have been the first clue for him, but I don't want to push.

I fully understand, I assure him as he slaps another one back and we get to talking about soul mates. Do soul mates meet in a bar? Could be I missed where we'd connected on that level over my gin and tonic.

I'm beginning to wane here . . . wax, too. I want to go home now. I don't want to sit up straight to be sure the girls are pointing northbound anymore. I'm tired and whiny, and I have no clue how to end this marathon of new-millennium dating phrases like *connected* and *feeling each other*.

I don't feel anything but exhausted, personally. Oh, wait, that's not true. I do *feel* very connected to my blankie, and I am definitely *feeling* my pillow. I decide to end my date if it's my last act on earth.

I mention the hour to Mr. Twelve-Step candidate, and he offers to walk me to my car. It's all downhill from here because I suddenly remember that a bit of slobber could be involved in this and I ain't playin' that.

I'm pretty quick, and now I thank the good Lord above for my sometimes mentally debilitating swirl of thought, 'cuz I'm ready for hot stuff. As we approach my car, I turn to him and stick my hand out. "Thanks, Fill-in-the-blank, I had a great time."

He shakes my hand and pulls me into an embrace that rivals the WWF.

"So what did you think?" he says into my neck.

I think I have to get home and take my miracle bra off or I'll implode. "Think?" I respond into his shoulder, where my lips are mushed.

"Yeah. What did you think of me?"

I struggle out of his embrace and do the old arm's-length thing. Did someone forget to give me the scorecard where I check off his assets so I can hold it up for him to see? Ya know, like on a scale of one to five wet panties, your conversational abilities are . . . I hesitate and then recuperate quite nicely, thank you. "I think you're very nice, Fill-in-the-blank," I respond.

He cocks his head at me and says, "So can I call you?"

Oh, no, no, no, a resounding no! "If you'd like to get together for a friendly cup of coffee sometime, sure, I'd love that," I offer as a condolence and the big fat hint that our Vegas wedding at Elvis's Chapel of Love is off.

"Friendly?" Fill-in-the-blank asks.

OK. I gotta split because Houston has a problem. "Yes, *friendly*. I had a great time, but I really think we're better off friends." The kiss of death for any man or woman.

Friends.

Let's just be friends, OK?

I quickly open my car door and say a hasty good-night to Fill-in-the-blank, who stands firmly rooted to the parking lot.

I'm not very good with confrontation. I hit 'em low and run away. Or drive—it varies from case to case.

However, I'm not feeling too bad, because this was a success as far as I'm concerned. I had a nice time, and the conversation, while not mind-boggling, was certainly pleasant.

As I tuck myself in that night, I decide this dating thing isn't horrible. I know my morals. I know my own code of date ethics. Ain't nobody gettin' the cookies in the cookie jar. Fill-in-the-blank reminded me of that. I feel very warm and fuzzy as I drift off to sleep.

Until the next day, of course, when I get a phone message from Fill-in-the-blank, who wants to get together again "real soon." We did exchange phone numbers. I mean, it was only on the off chance one of us flattened a tire on the highway on the way to our clandestine meeting. I click Delete because, as I said, I suck at confrontation.

I also check my e-mail again, which once more has my in-box jam-packed. I answer e-mail and continue to correspond with potential February 14th gift bearers.

And my journey continues. I joke with my girlfriends that this is a venture sadly out of control. I forward them e-mails from the men who wish to capture me like small prey. We laugh a lot. Sometimes we even sigh. I begin to book dates a week in advance with a waiting list of at least two days. Cancellation must occur on or prior to a twenty-four-hour period, or you will be billed.

No, I'm kidding.

I continue my manhunt, going on several dates in a week. I mean, what the hell, right? It's the whole "I feel pretty" theory. These men are like chocolate in a candy store. I want to try every damn variety. To a certain degree, I do.

I am now officially a date slut.

I'm exhausted. I begin not only to lose sleep but also to lose track of the names of men I'm due to meet—er, have met, will meet. I have Post-it notes on a calendar of the men I like and what I like about them, and if their names are the same, I label them by their online user ID. I answer the same questions over and over until my teeth hurt. The most popular being, Will you write about me in your next book? My response: Only if you're interesting enough.

I have the social life of Paris Hilton now, and still, each date I go on, I leave feeling either that I did all the talking while they stared blankly at me or that there just wasn't any chemistry.

Another biggie in the dating lingo—*chemistry.*

Either ya got it or ya don't.

Ten dates later and I don't. However, the guys I go out with do, or they are sadly misguided in Chemistry 101. I think part of the trouble is, I really am a good sport. Yes, for all my wisecracking, I can hang with anyone. I love people, and the writer in me loves to dig into their wee little minds. My dates leave feeling that I am a potential mate, and I leave feeling none of the above dating lingo, but I am getting out and having a great time meeting new people. I even consented to kiss one date because I did feel a bit of chemistry with him.

It was my first kiss in twenty-one years.

I was a nervous wreck. I had every right to be. I couldn't remember the last time my tongue did Pilates like that.

My date summation? I went to the movies, had drinks, dinner, and coffee, coffee, coffee.

I now know all of the Starbucks employees by first name and even their family members. We exchange Christmas cards.

But, thus far, I wasn't feeling connected, hooked up, or anything close to chemistry.

I wasn't discouraged. I liked my single existence. I was freer than I'd ever been. Captain-of-my-ship-type stuff and I didn't mind a bit. I told my editor that just recently. "I feel great," I said. "My life is pretty good, and I'm happy. I don't need anyone to

make me complete, but someone to share with would be great."
I meant it, too. My sons were thriving since my divorce. We had a great house, and my career was going well.

Then, as in the romance novels I write, I met someone who sorta broke the chain of the still-misunderstood-by-me dating lingo.

Yep, it happened. Chemistry, biology, trigonometry, you name it, he had it—all in one big old package. I was feeling him, and he was feeling me. We connected on every single level and a couple I think we invented.

I didn't go online to find a soul mate. I wasn't even in this to find a steady boyfriend, truthfully. I was in it to meet new people and discover the social life I never had because I married so young.

It was an experience that taught me something valuable: never compromise your ethics, never cross your personal boundaries, never give up on the belief that you deserve the best, but every once in a while, take a chance.

I liken it to being a skydiver waiting at the exit of an airplane: scary yet exhilarating. Sometimes you just gotta open the door and jump.

2.

Prince Charming = Santa Claus

(Happily) Giving Up Myths

She did observe, with some dismay, that, far from
conquering all, love lazily sidestepped practical problems.
—Joan Stafford

Marriage is a great institution, but I'm not
ready for an institution yet.
—Mae West

Detour

Debra Ginsberg

I'm in the car with G and we're driving south on Interstate 5. We're just outside San Francisco and headed all the way to San Diego, so we're at the beginning of this particular journey. Our other journey—the one we're on as a couple—is in its fifth year. I'm not sure what this length of time says about where we are in the relationship. I know it's the longest romantic relationship I've ever been in, but it's possible that we could be together another ten, twenty, even thirty years, in which case we'd look back on this time and consider it still the "beginning." But I'm over forty and so is G. We each have children in their late teens. He has two ex-wives and I have . . . a history of my own. It's difficult, at this stage of the game, to see anything, especially a relationship, as "new."

We travel well together, G and I. He's perpetually late, and I'm always too early. He packs more than he needs, and I never take enough. G often misplaces things like pens, tickets, and keys. I have a need, bordering on obsessive-compulsive, to check and recheck that I always have those items within easy reach. Between the two of us, we manage to strike a good balance. On the road, we always agree when to stop, what to eat, at which station to tune the radio.

It's the radio or, rather, the CD that inspires my next comment. Eric Clapton and B. B. King are singing together. "I want to marry you," the chorus goes. "Isn't that what you want, too?"

I settle my mostly finished coffee in one of the car's multiple cup holders and turn to G. He gives me a sweet smile from behind his hip shades. I check the speedometer. G, who drives thousands of miles a year for work, is doing eighty-five.

"So, G," I say, and clear my throat, "are we ever going to get married, or what?"

His reaction is instant. Foot lifted off gas—look of horror quickly replaced by a broad grin and strangled chuckle. He takes a couple of seconds to gather himself, during which time I can see the thoughts leaping across his face like sparks off a brush fire.

"I thought you didn't want to get married," he says finally. "Isn't that what you told me?"

"Yes," I answer. "I did say that. And I didn't want to. Then."

"And now?"

"And now. . ."

"And now you do," he finishes for me. "Because that's what all women want."

I fold my arms across my chest and sink back into the car seat, extremely annoyed at being reduced, again, to the stereotypical marriage-or-bust female I become whenever the word *marriage* comes up.

"I'm not the one with two ex-wives," I say huffily.

"See?" he says. "I rest my case."

"Come on," I tell him. "I'm serious. I want to talk about this seriously."

"You know how I feel about it," he says. "We've been over this."

"Have we?" I ask, but I already know the answer.

It's true; this is not the first time the M-word has come up in conversation between the two of us. We've skirted around it maybe a half dozen times before. And every time, G is able to get us off the topic with a skillful mix of jocularity and sincerity. He's so good at this kind of diversion that I still don't know how he really feels about marriage. Rather, I don't know how he really feels about marrying *me*. Or not marrying me, as the case may be. What I do know is that, from the very first days of our relationship, he has anticipated that I will want to get married. *All women*, as he's just said again, want to get married. And this, for G (and so many other men) is not necessarily a good thing. It's an attitude I've been fighting my entire single-female life.

As far back as I can remember, I've wanted only three things out of life: a husband, children, and time to write. The order and importance of these items have changed over the years, but they've always been there. Still, even as a very young child, I was cognizant enough to realize that I could write and produce children on my own. The husband part . . . well, I had to *get* one of those. I figured it was pretty simple, though, and I based this notion on the tale of the Frog Prince—my favorite fairy tale. Princess kisses frog (a very small sacrifice), and he instantly becomes perfect husband/prince. I was five years old when this idea first took hold, and for the better part of the next three decades, I held fast to the notion that inside every frog I kissed a potential prince loomed large.

Unfortunately, my mother did nothing to discourage this delusion of mine.

My mother believed in true love and in fated pairings. She believed that there was somebody intended just for me and that I would find him sooner rather than later. She even admitted to believing, at first, that the main purpose of my going to college was to find a husband. She believed, so definitely, in white horses, in princes, and in happily ever after. Even after decades of crash-and-burn relationships, when it seemed I'd proved beyond the shadow of a doubt that a frog is really just a frog and that no amount of kissing can change that, my mother still maintained, "You never know, he could still be out there."

But, although it would be awfully convenient, I can't lay full blame for my romantic missteps at my mother's feet. Her there's-a-soul-mate-for-everyone philosophy was passed down from her own mother, after all, and her mother's mother before that. And as for the things I wanted, I felt I had an absolute right to them. It was, I assumed, the natural order of things.

There were subtle cues all around me that not only reinforced this notion but also perpetuated it. I took some of these cues from TV shows such as *Love, American Style* and *I Dream of Jeannie*. The latter show in particular appealed to me. To this day, my favorite episodes are the ones in which Major Nelson proposes to Jeannie, followed by their wedding and honeymoon in her bottle. It's the pinnacle of Jeannie's life, this marriage. Finally she is validated and can appear in public. She becomes a real woman. I never stopped to consider that Jeannie was already all-powerful and could have blinked into existence anything she wanted—including Major Nelson—because wasn't it the ultimate dream come true to say "yes, oh yes" with the velvet box opened to reveal a sparkling solitaire, and the man down on one knee?

There was a catch to this dream, though. By the time I had graduated from high school, I knew that it wasn't cool or appropriate to want these things (or, at the very least, to admit wanting them). The women of my generation (post–baby boom, pre–generation X—"tweeners," as we are sometimes known) missed the bra-burning feminism of the early seventies but were left with its backlash. We were meant to be independent, educated, *and* beautiful—like the girls on *Charlie's Angels*, for example. We rejected what we saw as the crass materialism of the ring and the meaningless rituals of engagement and marriage—on the surface, at least. We were supposed to benefit from the struggles of our mothers and break the traditional molds set for dependent housewives.

Not surprisingly, casual sex never fell out of fashion in the same way. My peers and I came of age before AIDS hit hard and before the big swing back to "family values." The genie came out of the bottle for us and never felt like going back in. What this all meant, for me at least, was a truly confusing mix of signals. I was supposed to give my body freely, but I wasn't supposed to expect support or guidance from anyone I gave it to. In addition, if I considered myself truly liberated, I wouldn't even want any of those things.

But I did. So, too, did many of my peers. Outwardly, we scoffed at the conventions, but inwardly we bought into them. We wanted them.

My old friend Dave is a perfect example. In the months before it happened, Dave bubbled over with vitriol at the hoopla surrounding the marriage of Prince Charles and Lady Diana. He couldn't stop talking about how much time and money had been wasted on the whole affair and how this indicated that nobody knew what was really important anymore. Finally, when the wedding arrived, he stayed up all night to watch it on TV (as did *every woman I knew*). While he watched, he composed an epic poem about the event. It was a masterwork of bitterness and youthful indignation over what he felt was the ultimate moral travesty. About six years later, long before he turned thirty, Dave had a giant wedding of his own that was traditional, cheesy, and full of pomp and regalia. He even had an engagement period beforehand with a ring, invitations, the whole thing.

He'd found his princess.

Ultimately, almost every one of my college friends and acquaintances ended up getting engaged and married in traditional ways, although many of them waited until their thirties to do so. This was just further proof of what I had always suspected: the game stays the same; it's just the rules that change.

My confused notions of what marriage was supposed to be

all about led me down a very twisted road. And I ended up kissing way too many frogs. I did get engaged, get married, and have a child, but not in that order and not with the same man. My engagement ended when my fiancé wrestled me to the ground in a parking lot in an attempt to tear his ring from my finger. My "marriage" (a quickie Las Vegas job à la Britney Spears) lasted less than a year. As for my son's father, he took a powder months before the baby was born, never to return.

At about thirty-five, I finally gave up—and not in the fake "if I say I'm giving up, then maybe my prince will finally appear" kind of way, either. I was done with the whole thing. What really sealed it for me was that I discovered the *real* tale of the Frog Prince. The princess never kisses the frog, as it turns out. After the frog manipulates her into taking him up to her *bed* for a little "companionship," the princess hurls him at the wall, at which point he transforms into a prince. Well, I thought, if I'd known that from the beginning, I would have done things very differently indeed.

And then, at thirty-seven, I met G, and my thoughts about marriage shifted once again. Until I met him, I had come to a genuine acceptance of and comfort with being perpetually single. But my relationship with G is not only the longest, but also the most *normal* relationship I've ever had with a man. Part of that has something to do with how old we are and the lives we've already led. But part of it also has to do with the fact that, after running circles around the idea of marriage, I have finally come to an understanding of what it should be. And this has nothing to do with princes, white dresses, or china patterns, but everything to do with partnership, friendship, and, yes, love. I don't know how to explain any of this to G in a way that won't make him default— again—to his all-women-want-to-get-married philosophy.

So, instead, I just say something ridiculous. "I just feel stupid calling you my boyfriend," I tell him. "At my age."

G considers this for a moment. "I'll get you a ring," he says at last. "And you can call me your husband if that's all it is. But to get married . . . I just don't think. . ."

He peers out the windshield, leaning forward in his seat.

"Don't think what?" I ask.

"I don't think we're going in the right direction," he says. "Look at the sign."

I look up as we pass the sign that says Welcome to Stockton, which means that we're not going south at all. In fact, if we're in Stockton, we've gone a hundred miles north, in the wrong direction.

We're both laughing as we turn around and prepare to try to make up the time. It's all my fault, G maintains. This is what happens when you start talking about marriage—you wind up in Stockton, for heaven's sake. "Make sure," he says, "that when you tell this story, because I know you will, you add that it was all because of *you*. How can I be expected to navigate when I'm talking about marriage?"

And, of course, we are no longer talking about marriage at all. We're racing south, trying to get home before it gets too late and trying not to think about how much time we've wasted on our detour.

An hour or two after our rapid turnaround, when I'm sure we're back on track, I decide to make one more attempt. "So are we finished with that conversation?" I ask G.

"For now," he says. "Unless you want to wind up in Oregon."

"Right," I say. "Got it."

I lean my head against the window, preparing to sink back into my own jumbled thoughts, but G won't let me drift. He reaches over and takes my left hand in his right and doesn't let go. He holds on to me like that until we get to Los Angeles and he needs both of his hands to steer.

never again

Merrill Markoe

Sprawled here on the rocky fjord of middle age, I can see the landscape of my life laid out before me. Back there on the horizon are the precipitous cliffs of my teenage years. That extinct volcano next to them was my early twenties. And to the northwest . . . that big bombed-out open field full of trenches and barbed wire that resembles the remnants of the Battle of Verdun from World War I? That is my love life. They say love makes the world go round, which goes a long way toward explaining why the world is tottering toward an apocalyptic mess.

Ah, love. What a pain in the ass it has been for most of my life. That creepy sick feeling of obsession and elation produced by an unexpectedly intense moment of chemistry with a member of the opposite sex you've just met. Followed by the anxiety, the turmoil, the misunderstandings and inappropriate expectations, then the confusion and the inevitable sadness and disappointment that come from being thrust into a state of emotional and physical intimacy with a complete stranger. Couple that with the fun of finding out that the two of you are at cross-purposes on just about everything, since not only do you not agree on mutual goals, let alone even the definition of the relationship you don't exactly share, but he also appears to have a personality disorder, a substance-abuse problem, or, for bonus points, a criminal record.

In my past, I had three long-term (more than three years, but less than eleven) "love" relationships, all vying for the title of most deranged. At no point did I seriously pursue marriage within any of them, since their obvious shortcomings made a vow of "forever" seem insane. But, interestingly enough, having a clear picture of their limitations did not seem to keep me from moving in with these men and sticking around for a long time. Because in my checkered youth, living with a nutty guy made the same kind of common sense as having sex on the second date.

By the time the last of these aforementioned relationships ended, I was such a quaking mass of colliding, exploding neurotransmitter malfunctions that the only coherent sentence I could form in my native tongue went: "Never again."

So there I was, afloat in the late 80s and drowning in my late thirties. Ah, the late 80s! Those happy-go-lucky days when single women were all luxuriating in that delightful study that claimed that the chances of a woman in her forties getting kidnapped by a terrorist were greater than her chances of getting married. Perhaps the only remotely beneficial by-product of 9/11 was the instant and radical change in the terrorist-kidnapping odds . . . in favor of older single women.

And this despite the fact that Mother Nature, in her infinite wisdom, never intended for her daughters, or any of her other children, to keep dating for decades. Since the time between meeting and mating in pretty much every other species can be measured in hours, if not minutes or seconds, it's pretty clear that Mother Nature's original plan for humans went something like this: A teenage girl marries the first available man she lays eyes on who can provide food and shelter for their future family. Then, whatever sequence of events transpires from that point on, including wife and child abuse or incest, is to be filed under the rubric "happy marriage."

Of course this is slightly at odds with the wisdom of our current culture, where thirty has become "postadolescent," and forty is "just a kid getting started." We live in the first period of American history in which two-thirds of the adults feel that they are barely out of their teens. And not surprisingly, this delusional group has altered the definition of a happy marriage to mean a relationship in which both parties are giddy with love day and night. And if a partner becomes Grumpy or Sleepy or Dopey (or any of the seven dwarfs except Happy), a Greek chorus of friends and relatives steps forward to chant: "You don't need this crap. You deserve more. Pack up and leave." Small wonder that the available dating pool of singles has expanded to include pretty much everyone except grade-school kids and the embalmed.

So now it's no longer unusual for men and women in their forties, fifties, sixties, and even older to be trolling for dates. (And I use the word *troll* intentionally, since appropriate candidates are generally not as appealing as they were the last time anyone looked.)

And of these so-called appropriate candidates, it comes as no surprise to anyone that a percentage of the older males prefer to pursue much younger women. But there is a less discussed additional reason that geezers like youngsters. I'm referring to the fact that young women, bless their little pinheads, are frequently under the impression that everything that goes wrong in a relationship is their fault. They still believe that once the word *love* is on the table, anything untoward can be fixed by just figuring out the right thing to say, or do, or wear.

Conversely, women have by their midthirties generally been to therapy, read a few self-help books, or watched a lot of *Oprah*. They have given serious thought to collating the lessons of their mistakes in an effort not to repeat them. Thus, they stare grim-faced, eyes rolling, when men their own age try to recycle the same repertoire of relationship stunts and bullshit they got away with in their twenties. "You're not serious" are not the three words these men want to hear.

In my own case, after my last relationship ended, I had taken in so much therapeutic advice via shrinks, books, and radio shows that from the moment I laid eyes on a new man, I would begin mentally cataloguing his tics and flaws. By the time he spoke a full sentence, I would have him filed by psychological illness and emotional dysfunction. I would have decided if he was narcissistic or sociopathic, a substance abuser, depressive or bipolar, an obsessive-compulsive, a hysteric, a neurotic, or a delightful combination of them all. I would be looking for the iceberg tips of dangerous issues lurking in his tone of voice on my answering machine.

And so specific were my criteria that for the next twelve years I shared my home with only a large herd of dogs and their tumbleweed-sized wads of free-floating hair. I saw myself as a kind of canine Jane Goodall (but minus all the tedious research).

In those years of solitude, I tried to pursue a life of peace, maturity, and self-esteem (by which I mean I attempted to set the limit at two despondent statements per day about "not having a life" and one pathetic, transparently unsuitable affair with an inadequate attractive man per month). Because I had a great tolerance for solitude, I was able to deal with this lifestyle pretty well until I hit critical mass and had to admit that I really did want to be a part of another tiny unit of humans. Even if they were destined to hurt me or make me a nervous wreck.

So I morphed my edict of "Never again" into "Never again will I live with a man unless we get married," my thinking being that if I could take that additional step, I would have crossed from the minority who choose the anarchy of living together to the safer territory of the majority, with their divorces, lawsuits, and mutual restraining orders.

Someplace in the middle of all this, I made the acquaintance of a man with whom I exchanged e-mails every day for two years. These e-mails were often the highlight of my day. Therefore, I had no hesitation about starting to date him when he eventually turned up single. (And when I say "date," I mean wake up at two in the morning to cook him dinner and, of course, have sex with him.)

Interestingly, I found that falling in love in my forties was a very different experience than at any other point. To begin with, it felt a little like tiptoeing barefoot over a frozen pond into a dense, dark forest, hoping to make it to the cozy cabin without being buried in an avalanche or unexpectedly tumbling into a snowy ravine.

Whereas younger love is mainly about potential (and about the illusion of magical transformations that might occur when people unexpectedly come to their senses), as you get older you learn that expecting a person to magically change for the better makes as much sense as counting on the lottery for next month's rent.

You also learn that love attraction is often based on repetition compulsion, wherein a person is attracted to a duplicate of a powerful child-parent relationship (good or bad). And since it's a door that swings both ways, if he is *your* repetition compulsion, *you* are also *his*. That is why, for the relationship to have a prayer of succeeding, both new significant repetition compulsions had better be not just cognizant of the obstacle course but have some experience with how it is run. Unfortunately, this is not so easy to accomplish, because oddly enough, most people think that in any relationship, only the other person is the problem.

My new later-in-life gentleman caller stood out immediately as different. First of all, the final act in any previous relationship argument was always "OK, then GET OUT." Now, suddenly even irrational fights ended with a discussion that contained adult perspective, insight, and a path to resolution. Also, after many years of therapy, I'd learned how to hold my own ground rather than agree that everything was my fault, apologize, unilaterally disarm, then pout and pretend that nothing had ever happened. Or failing that, have rashes, stomachaches, and asthma.

As I got older, I also began to realize that there is no real reason to seek and import chaos, since life itself is inherently chaotic. And that the most rebellious, defiant act imaginable is to somehow create and maintain a pleasurable, peaceful little corner of the world that fits you perfectly.

And so it came to pass that almost three years into this relationship, aware that it continued to grow in a good direction, when my gentleman caller's landlord decided to sell the house he was renting, I heard my mouth speaking the words, "Why don't you move in with me?" But even as I did, I could feel my face flush and terror stab my heart as I was swallowed up in a cyclone of images from the last moments of previous relationships: the lying, the swearing, the screaming, the vitriol, the day I filled his car with his clothes and had it removed from the premises. Yet despite this frightening montage, there I was one day, helping him pack his belongings into cardboard boxes from Staples. What about my edict? I silently wondered. What ever happened to never living with another man unless I felt enough of a commitment to get married?

"I'm going to sit down and really give it all some thought," I said to myself, even as I continued to help him pile his boxes into my car, fill out his forwarding-address cards, and add his books to my bookshelves.

But as I was throwing out some of my snow globes to make room for his gigantic assortment of Napoleons, I heard myself putting my edict aside for the time being. "Hell, why rush into anything?" I was saying. "OK, three years is a long time. But it's not all THAT long." Turns out that my relationship edicts are eerily like my New Year's resolutions. So where edicts are concerned . . . Never again.

Now it's three and a half years later, and things continue going well. Though I'll admit I'm bugged by how stupid the word *boyfriend* sounds in the last half of your life. And I guess if we're still not married by the time I croak, they won't mention him in my obituary. (If I even get an obituary long enough to include any details of my life besides a mention of Stupid Pet Tricks.)

And ultimately, here is the best thing I have learned: that the good part of having had a checkered past is that when you're older, if you paid attention, you're really good at checkers.

Remember me?

Liz Byrski

"**R**emember me?" he asks, on the telephone from the other side of the world. And I remembered because I had never really forgotten.

"But it's such a long time."

"Thirty-seven years, and there hasn't been a day when I haven't thought about you," he says.

We had met in England in 1962. I was eighteen, a well-behaved, middle-class, submissive convent girl. He was thirty-two, divorced, German, but had made his home in California some years earlier. Now he was working in England. We fell in love.

"Marry me?" he asked a few months later when it was time for him to leave. "Come back with me to California?"

"Yes!" I said.

"No!" said my parents. "We like him but. . ." But what? Too old, too divorced, too German, too soon, too young, too risky, too far away from us. "Wait a year, and then we'll see."

We wept and parted. We waited. We wrote long, loving letters until one day, without explanation, he ended it.

"Thank goodness we didn't let you go," my parents said.

"We told you so," friends said. "An older man, divorced . . . hhmm!"

I was sure it must have been my fault. Obviously, I was not good enough, not clever, pretty, smart enough. Time passed, months, years, decades, but I never forgot. He was my first love, the love that never had to stand the test of living together, of children and money troubles, of work and boredom and aging. He was the love against whom all others were measured and found wanting. Lost love, the sweetest love of all. And now, two marriages and various relationships later, here he is on the telephone.

"You were—still are—the love of my life," he says. "I've been looking for you for twelve years, even employed a detective to find you. Finally I went to your old home, traced you through the owner."

Twenty years earlier I moved to Australia, and I am on holiday in England when I get his call. Two weeks later, after daily transatlantic conversations, he flies from San Francisco to meet me in Germany before I return to Australia.

"We'll need a password," he says, "in case we don't recognize each other."

"I'll recognize you."

"You might not. I'm sixty-eight, an old man now. The password is 'thirty-seven years.'"

Caught in the magic of the impossible dream, I stare intently from the aircraft window as it makes its descent to Frankfurt. He's down there somewhere waiting for me. Will he think I'm too old, too fat, too outspoken, too different, too . . . everything?

Of course we recognize each other, just as we had recognized each other in that first glance across the lounge room of a north London apartment all those years ago. Chemistry is chemistry, but of course it doesn't *have* to be destiny unless one chooses to make it so. I choose it now, just as I chose it then, although he is not as I expected; he's older, of course, and older than his years, but attractive and surprisingly familiar. The arrivals hall empties around us, and we are still holding each other, searching each other's eyes, speechless with wonder at this extraordinary reunion. But I'm also uneasy.

"I hope I'm kissing the right person," I say, attempting levity to calm myself. "What's the password?"

"What password?" he asks in genuine surprise.

"How can I be serious about a person who forgets his own password?"

"You just have to remember that I came back," he says. "I always loved you, and I finally found you again."

I take the bait, he reels in his catch, and I am shamelessly thrilled to be caught.

A couple of hours later in a hotel room we are still crying, discussing the overwhelming possessiveness that led him to end it for fear that I would not be faithful to him. And then, cautiously at first, we make love for the first time in our lives. Thirty-seven years ago we were waiting until we were married.

And so the relationship is consummated and the anticipation and excitement fades into peaceful sleep . . . almost.

"You really have put on weight," he says, and the chill of his words brushes my neck. "I didn't expect you to be so heavy. I remember you used to be so beautiful, so slender."

And, of course, I am wide awake again, my acres of flesh vibrating with hurt, with fear of rejection. I move defensively away, but he doesn't notice because now he's asleep.

My greatest fear had been that he would think me too fat, and I had warned him that I was not the slim girl he remembered. He told me he loved big women, that as a boy he gazed for hours at pictures of robust women in underwear advertisements in his mother's magazines. I'm certainly robust but not huge: size 18, 172 pounds. I exercise regularly and am reasonably fit.

He had confided that *his* greatest fear was that I would think him too old, and of course I had noticed his slim but untoned body, soft wrinkled flesh, muscle wasting, loss of hair, and all the other signs of aging in a man who had not looked after himself. But my training in the art of preserving the male ego is easily revived. I keep my mouth shut. I tell myself I am being ridiculous, oversensitive; after all, he has been looking for me for twelve years, has traveled halfway around the world to meet me. Abandon yourself to love. And those uncomfortable little stabs of unease at the airport and now here in the bed? Well, you're so picky and critical. He's a charming, handsome man, and he wants *you*. Be thankful. So now it seems that my mother is in bed with us.

The next day we walk through operatic sets masquerading as German villages cloaked in snow. We hold hands, reminisce, inhale the romantic splendor of the landscape. Our breath floats in clouds as we walk the steep hill to a castle.

"Come along," he says, "come along, keep up. Got to get you fit. My, you *are* puffing."

I explain a medical condition which, irrespective of fitness levels, leaves me constantly short of breath. I cannot walk briskly and talk at the same time.

"We'll get some of that weight off you, and then you'll see," he says. "I once got a girlfriend to shed three stones. I'll soon have you slimmed down."

I keep walking and try not to think about what I'm hearing.

A couple of hours later we are sitting in a café drinking German coffee with cream in front of an open fire. Low beams, old etchings, coffee in a silver pot, *Glühwein* in tiny glasses, the glow of the cold air still flushing our cheeks—how fortunate I am to be here in this extraordinary romantic adventure. But the god of love is not the only one shooting arrows; the goddess of reason is getting in on the act. I realize he's been talking for ages, not *to* me but *at* me, and he's been doing it all day. Monologues. I'm bored. *Yes, dear, but that's because you're so picky and critical; he's a brilliant man. Clearly your father and I were wrong all those years ago. Yes, Mom.*

It's unfortunate that at this time I have not yet read Martha Gellhorn's warning written after her 1964 attempt to discover the new Germany. Young Germans, she wrote, "are taught to memorize facts but are not guided to relate facts, experience, observation, and emotion to produce their own personal thought." Lacking the legendary Martha's cool insight, I am blinded by his recitation of information, blinded to its lack of context, analysis, or thoughtful interpretation. And I have conveniently forgotten all those times other men have bored me with their monologues and that I have observed them boring other women speechless in cafés and restaurants. I'm seduced by this pseudointellect; even through my boredom it seems sexy because, after all, this man loves me. He came back.

On our second night together I teeter perilously on the tightrope of indecision when, waking, I see him silhouetted against the moonlit rectangle of the bedroom window.

"I have a confession to make," he says, climbing back into bed. My heart pounds with fear of what is to be revealed. "How would you feel if I told you I have a drug habit?"

My chest tightens; my mouth goes dry. To what can a sixty-eight-year-old be addicted? He's a bit hyper—coke perhaps? Speed? For a few seconds the god of love is suspended, and the goddess takes over. Here is my chance to extricate myself, beat a dignified retreat, retain the status of the unattainable beloved while freeing myself from my unease about the way this is developing. He is about to offer me a gracious and dignified escape route in which I will retain the luxury of the high moral ground.

"What do you mean? What drug?"

He circles me with his arms, his beard brushes my shoulder, and I feel his tears on my cheek.

"Your love," he says. "I am addicted to your love, and now that I've found you, I'm scared. I need your love like a drug. But there was someone else once, she found such love a burden, a millstone. Perhaps you. . ."

Me? No way, Jose! Love? I can take it. Love? Addicted to my love? I can handle that, baby, no worries. I've had relationships with alcoholics and workaholics, spent lonely nights longing for them to transfer their addiction from the booze or the job to me. And in that one hara-kiri moment I leap from the tightrope, and my mother sighs with relief. The past is put right. At last I have a man who is worthy of me, who is, by his own admission, addicted to me. Now she can really rest in peace . . . and me? Well, I can rest in . . . in what? Well, love, of course.

We reach the end of this stolen interlude, and he urges that we change our plans and stay another week. He cannot, he says, bear to part again. We must plan for the future. Cupid is still in the ascendant; reason and experience are denied life support. Desperate to be what he wants me to be, I rein in my caustic tongue, my cutting humor, my cynicism about love, romance, relationships. He has connected me to that elusive memory—myself when young. I am the perfect woman, indeed the perfect Aryan woman. He tells me so: fair hair, blue eyes, modest, quiet, and sweet-natured. I am eighteen again, except for the weight, but he'll soon get rid of that. Seduced by his fantasy, I am shocked when I see my reflection in a shop window. Who *is* that middle-aged woman?

It's my birthday, and he takes me shopping. He buys me not the gift I want, which is a simple piece of unusual, inexpensive silver jewelry, but what he wants me to have: ridiculously expensive and ornate German porcelain, which he loves, and which has to be insured and shipped back to Australia for safety. (It arrives two months later and costs me a considerable amount to clear through customs.) I've never been interested in porcelain and hate ornate patterns, but he has such good taste; at heart he is an artist, so he must be right.

So now I am feigning an interest not only in porcelain, but also in the stock market, power generation, and military history, subjects that raise a yawn at the very thought. But he wants me to be interested; indeed, he's injured by the slightest suggestion that these might not be universally fascinating subjects. As I fall asleep during that second week, Mom reminds me that I cannot expect him to be interested in my passions if I do not make an effort to be interested in his. But he's *not* interested in human rights, spirituality, left-wing politics, or literature. He *is* interested in books, but I soon discover that he's interested only in the ones he's read, which are on porcelain, the stock market, power generation, and military history.

And it's strange that when there is a pause in the monologue and I feel it's my turn to speak, it always seems to coincide with his urgent need to go to the bathroom, order another drink, or suggest we continue the conversation in the car, some other place, some other time. Martha, where were you when I needed you to tell me that the German "inability to put themselves in the place of others, even briefly, is like being blind and deaf . . . everything returns to them." But is it his Germanness or the simple fact that he is a man, and a man of a certain age? Whatever—Cupid is on overtime and edges me further down the slope into the abyss of self-deception.

We have survived thirty-seven years of separation and two weeks together. Now we separate again in a parting as poignant and painful as the first one. We fly away from each other, he back to California, me to Western Australia—literally as far apart as it is possible to be on this earth. And it feels as though a part of me has been ripped away. I am terrified to step back into my life; I fear it may swallow me and that I will never find my way out and back to him. I am as frightened of losing him as I was thirty-seven years ago.

"Remember me?" he asks again over the phone. "Do you think I looked for you all those years just to lose you again?"

Everything has changed; the center of life has shifted. I will do what I should have done thirty-seven years ago. I will go to California to be with him, embrace this wondrous second chance to live the love I lost.

And, of course, in the few months before I leave Australia I will ignore those arrows that the goddess keeps firing. I will crush my unease about opinions and beliefs so at odds with my own, about his self-obsession and his intolerance of questions that challenge him. From the other side of the world his very existence dominates my life. I can't write, I can't work, I can only relive the past, obsess about what might have been and what will now be.

The first sight of the Golden Gate Bridge stops my breath. I am part of a movie: that red bridge, the Bay, Alcatraz, Twin Peaks, Tony Bennett, pastel-toned buildings scattered across the hillsides as if by the hand of a friendly giant. Now I am in love with a city, too. And then there is Berkeley: houses clinging perilously to the escarpment, red-gold leaves scattered on sidewalks, the smell of wood smoke, crisp fall mornings, and mist clouding the Bay Bridge. I am drunk with excitement, glamour, and the vibrant sense of history: UC Berkeley, the Black Panthers, Gertrude and Alice, the Beats, the Grateful Dead, Janis, the Castro, Jack London, everything, and all thanks to him.

Time passes, and my love affair with California grows as my love affair with him becomes increasingly dependent on not being myself. I exist in his fantasy. My own fantasy about a passionate, loving relationship based on equality and respect for each person's individuality has been replaced by the masquerade of my role in his movie. I'm performing a spectacular audition for the role of perfect wife, adopting hated domestic routines, agreeing with him when I don't agree, deferring to his judgment when he is clearly mistaken or ill informed. I am even apologizing when he accuses me of flirting with a waiter or smiling at a bartender. I am a hideous throwback to my eighteen-year-old self, and it is unforgivable, because then I did not know any better and now I do.

He was in the Hitler Youth and talks frequently of "the great betrayal" of 1945, when he discovered that this wonderful movement was a cover for evil. But although he pays lip service to equality, he does not live it. His negative messages about my body size continue to chip away at my self-esteem, and in silent secret protest I eat outrageously and put on weight. It is my one feeble act of resistance. *Fat* is an abusive adjective. When he relates a dispute with a bank teller, a waitress, a female security officer, they are "fat bitches" even when they are slim. I hold my tongue. How can I explain the significance of this meta-language? But when they are "fat black bitches," I challenge him. My challenge is taken as a personal insult, but I always knew it would be. Why else have I kept my mouth shut so long?

Thirty-seven years ago he was too far left for my parents' comfort, and I didn't even know what *left* and *right* meant. Now I'm a feminist socialist and to me he is a far-right conservative, while to himself he is a small-L liberal.

I frequently lift the phone to book my flight home, but then hold off because, unbelievably, a part of me still hopes, still wonders if it's all my fault. When my visa expires and I do leave, I am devastated and feel lost back home. A few months later, just over a year since we met in Frankfurt, he comes to Australia, and I introduce him to my home, my family and friends. I am schizophrenic. In his world I can just about survive his fantasy, survive being what he wants. In my world it is unbearable. My friends watch me as they might if I had just gone through a sex change. I am unraveling in front of them, but it is nothing as bad as what they now realize has been happening for the past year. I am unmasked, and he has no idea it's happening. When, after three months, he suggests staying on, I push him to leave, and when he does, I am at first hugely relieved, then devastated by my own behavior, then crushed with exhaustion and disappointment.

And so at last I listen to my true self, and I begin to probe the past. Mostly I do it by e-mail. I need it in writing because I know that he will lie outrageously when it suits him. I need to know I am not imagining his dishonesty, that I am not insane, as I am beginning to suspect.

I discover that just six weeks after he ended it with me in 1962, he married someone else, someone he had not even met at the time he wrote that last letter. I discover that a few years before I took his first "Remember me?" call, he had been back to Germany to find the girl he had loved as a teenager. She, too, had been the love of his life, the only one, and although she resisted his fantasy, he called her daily, pestered her to meet him, begged her to go with him to California. Finally, I discover that the seductive tale of his twelve-year search for me was fantasy too, as were the trips to England to find me and the private detective. One day, during a business trip to England, he had simply inquired at my old home and struck it lucky with the generosity of the current owner. When I point out the power of his lies in shaping my response to his phone calls, he doesn't understand.

"But I love you," he says. "I tried to find you. You were always the love of my life."

It is useless to attempt to get him to understand the subtleties of what has happened between us, the hideous manipulation, the deception, and the sexual politics.

He has lied to me, deliberately misled me. But is what he has done worse than what I have done? I have convinced him that I am what he wants. I have acted out his fantasy, and he has no idea who I really am. I am a chameleon; I am a sickening creature. And very soon I am sick, devastatingly sick. I am clinically depressed; I have a thyroid condition and chronic fatigue. I can barely move. For almost two years there are long periods when I cannot work. I am so exhausted I can barely hold a book. I cannot earn my living, look after my garden, pay my mortgage. I sell my house and downsize to an apartment. It's beautiful and peaceful and, best of all, he has never been here. I struggle back to life, to work, to myself. He has no idea what this has done to me, and I can't explain, because he could never understand. And I can't blame him, for I entered willingly into the fantasy. Besides, if I tell him, he will make himself a victim. He will say that he is the world's greatest dreamer, a romantic fool, that his thoughts are only of me and my happiness, that he worries about me and the worry makes him ill. And once again I will have to resist the temptation to reflect him back, not as the person he is, but as a romantic hero, twice his actual size.

Slowly I break the cycle of codependence, stop him from calling me, reduce the flow of e-mails, stop reacting, stop disclosing things about my life, stop feeding the fantasy, stop trying to explain.

Once again I am a single woman of a certain age. I come and go as I choose and answer to no one. I stay up late at night and stay home on weekends. I write when it suits me, have coffee or breakfast with my friends, go to the movies on the spur of the moment, stay in bed, talk on the phone. Shop for the things I want, eat when I choose, and rarely cook. I iron naked in the kitchen when I need something to wear. I am at last my own person, free of the fear that I am alone because I am unlovable and free of the illusion that I am the love of someone's life. Despite my age and considerable personal growth, there are things about myself that I have not managed to change, and now I really can't be bothered to try. I have made many mistakes with men, and with this one I compounded them all. I was a solitary only child, and now I am a solitary older person. A single woman of a certain age, and I love it.

[*The Martha Gellhorn quotes are from "Is There a New Germany?,"* Atlantic Monthly, *February 1964.]*

Beaks Benedict

Ms. Gonick

Who knew I wouldn't meet my first man until I was in my late forties? Not I. I thought that I'd met all kinds of them—I'd even lived with a few—and that having entered the crone zone (that one-way boulevard all women who don't die first must travel), I'd given them up for good. Ha! That's like thinking you've given up chocolate when all you ever tasted was carob. If you don't know what carob is, just ask a hippie. Don't ask a man, though. Do not ask Mack.

I was taking my octogenarian parents out for their midmorning hobble the day we met Mack just outside his ranch. I hadn't even known they lived near a ranch until I became their unqualified caregiver and sort of moved myself into their house. That's the joy of being a writer; it's a job you can fail at from anywhere. I didn't even need to bring my computer, just my toothbrush, notebook, and hair shirt. Since caregiving is a job you can't *succeed* at from anywhere (Nature, let's face it, is working against you), a hair shirt makes the best uniform.

With a parent's arm hooked onto each elbow, I inched them slowly down the big road that eventually led to a T by a fence. When you're over eighty (or just new to the crone zone), it helps to have a destination that precedes the big D, and for us it was the goats who lived at (no pun intended) the end of the road. Since it helps to have a purpose as well, I decreed ours to be bringing them lunch. When she's not working against you, Nature also works for you, by providing odd animals for oldsters to feed. That was my thinking, anyway. My dad was recovering from an obnoxious back surgery, my mom from an even more obnoxious post-traumatic stress disorder (she'd lost thirty pounds after driving her car through a restaurant's front window), and *my* purpose was to get them to feel better fast. Or just to act as though they felt better, so that I could.

"Yer gonna git yer hand chewed off," said a male voice as my father stuck the first of his carrots into the lunatic face of a goat.

"I'd like to see him try it!" retorted my father. He didn't know who he was talking to, but since when do retired attorneys care about that? The point for them is the talking. No, in fact, the point is the arguing. This was the itchiest hair on my shirt—his constant refuting of whatever I said, even if I just said, "Hello."

"Naw. You gotta do it like this," said the voice, and that's when I thought I saw Yosemite Sam—a flesh-and-blood version—heading our way. Gently but firmly, he broke the carrot into small pieces, flattened my dad's palm, and lay the pieces on it.

"This way he can slurp it right up," he explained.

The goat indeed slurped it up.

"Kinda tickles, don't it?" he said.

Don't it? I thought.

But my father was giggling. I mean it. Giggling.

"Wanna try it, ma'am?" Yosemite said then to my mother. The sun on his belt buckle blinded us both, it being the size of a Buick.

My mother, who says no to everything always, could not even utter the word. She just backed away in testosterone horror. I was afraid she was going to fall down right there, but Yosemite caught her up by the waist.

"All righty, then," he said, with a nod. Then he turned this smile on me. "Kin I borrow yer dad fer a minute?"

"What for?" I asked suspiciously.

"His name's Harry," my mother said, finding her voice.

"Mine's Mack," he replied. "Say, Harry, wanna come feed my horse?" He might as well have asked if my dad wanted to visit Europe again, or go to a strip club, or whatever it is that men over eighty still want to do. Harry gave Mack his arm and they trundled uphill.

"Don't hurt him!" I yelled at their backs.

"Relax, daughter," he yelled. *Daughter?* "I'll have him back home in twenty."

You arrogant twit, I thought.

"You don't know where we live!" I yelled.

"Don't Harry?" he yelled.

Oh, right. I could hear Harry already, starting to tell Mack a limerick, one that I'd heard maybe six thousand times, and I was, I just realized, for once being spared. The next thing I heard was Mack laughing, then this question shouted over his shoulder:

"You gals like fresh eggs?"

His shoulder, too, was the size of a Buick. Both of them were. They were frightening.

"Sure, who don't?" I shouted back.

"Fresh eggs," mused my mother, who'd not eaten breakfast since the day she'd made headlines crashing into the restaurant. Its shattered window had made so much noise raining down on her car she'd thought she'd been caught in a spontaneous hailstorm— in Minnesota, unfortunately, which is not where we live. Now she tugged at my arm. "Is there bacon at home?"

The last bacon she'd bought had turned motley green, as had everything else in their fridge before I'd tossed it in horror, except for the greens, which had turned motley black. I told her I hadn't bought bacon since.

"I've got some," yelled Mack from the top of the hill. I swear, I thought I had just heard from God. And when I turned around and saw that Mack had gotten Harry—Harry who'd been felled by sciatica and just resurrected—on top of a horse, I knew that I had. Or from the devil, depending on whether Harry fell off or not.

"Don't look," I told my mother, and we both hobbled home.

When I say Mack was the first man I'd met, do I mean I don't have a man for a father? No, Harry's a man, all right, but as a sports-phobic Jewish lawyer violinist, he was never a man of American legend. Or, if he was, it was not the same American legend evoked by Mack's double negatives and cowboy boots. Not that this legend had ever attracted me; I thought it illiterate, uncultured, and base and only liked men who seemed, well, "evolved." My father, for instance, was too evolved to bother with car maintenance, which is why, before he gave me a car he no longer drove, he didn't get a mechanic to check it out first.

"Did you know this car has almost no brakes left?" a boy who was driving it asked me.

"Oh," I said. "Is it supposed to?"

I should have married that boy, whoever he was, but I probably thought he cared too much about car brakes to be a good match for me. I wanted men to be handsome and word smart and to have, like me, a vacuum for values. And so they did, which is why it really wasn't so painful ending up all alone in the crone zone. Did I really miss being with men who made fun of Anaïs Nincompoop's husband because they revered Henry Miller? No, I was better off sneaking Ensure into piña coladas to keep my mother from wasting away and playing Scrabble incessantly to keep my father from telling me limericks. At least I was doing someone some good before I met my own big D at the end of my personal crone zone. I'd even rewritten my epitaph. Instead of saying, "She Loathed Henry Miller," it'd say: "She Drove Her Parents to Their Doctors' Appointments."

And that might help make up for the rest of the mess.

How macho was Mack? Macho enough to pick up my father's forty-ton desk and move it across the room without help. And then, after Harry decided the first location really was better, to move it back without showing impatience. Every time he went out of our house he took the garbage out with him, and every time he came in he found something to fix and then fixed it. He'd either been, or still was, a trapper and skinner of bears, boxer and bouncer, reform-school graduate turned rodeo cowboy, high-rise construction worker, master carpenter, and search-and-rescue-team volunteer. He'd never heard of Shakespeare or Freud, never mind that wuss, Henry Miller. Depending on the decade, he'd been stabbed, beaten, pulverized, hospitalized, divorced, or abandoned, yet all of his daughters drove cars with good brakes. He himself owned and drove about six hundred vehicles (campers, horse trailers, motorcycles, the inevitable pickup truck), including an enormous red convertible Cadillac that looked, when driven, like a traveling blood clot. Which sort of made sense since that was the car Mack used to drive my parents to their doctors' appointments. Noting that I was a complete nervous wreck, he thought I should sit in back with my mother instead of up front, where, as soon as my father started a limerick, I'd lose my mind and kill everyone.

I re-revised my epitaph: "Mack Drove Her Parents to Their Doctors' Appointments. But Remember This: He Did It for Her."

I was not one iota attracted to him. His utter indifference to the written word not only repulsed me, it scared me. Also, he was a born-again Christian (Harry was the "first Jew" he'd ever met), and, dare I say it, he'd voted for Bush. Then there was the Yosemite Sam situation. That's how I still saw him: as a cartoon. Plus, he'd spent his whole life with his face in the sun and looked, to me, like Yosemite Senior. I would just as soon have kissed his heinous red rooster, the one responsible for the fresh eggs that he had, as promised, brought back with Harry the first day we'd met.

"Fry 'em up, daughter," he'd said, indicating the sea of bacon grease he already had sizzling in a pan on our stove. My parents were conked out in the living room.

"Stop calling me that," I'd said in a snit, sure he'd just crippled my father for life. Then I broke an egg open over the grease and screamed. There were streaks of blood and a quasi-formed beak.

"Good God, it's Rosemary's baby," I said.

That's when he'd told me he was a Christian and preferred my not taking the Lord's name in vain.

"Shut up," I said, cracking another egg open, only to see more blood and beak. I thanked God my mother was sleeping, because if she'd been watching, her appetite would have been squelched for all time.

"Now what?" I said, looking at Mack.

"Hard to say," he said, shrugging. "Beaks Benedict?"

It was the hardest I'd ever laughed in that kitchen, except for the time my lentil soup exploded because I hadn't covered the blender, and then I'd been drunk on piña coladas.

I loathe all sports and outdoor endeavors, but he taught me to ride a horse anyway. I guess I figured I was so old already that it didn't matter if it stepped on my head. What was I going to miss? My own future case of sciatica? Losing my license when I, too, drove through a restaurant, except that I, having forgotten to marry or have children, would then have to take the bus by myself, where young thugs would thrash me with my own walker?

What was so bad about the big D anyway? Mack seemed to have no problem with it. He showed me, on horseback, where all the dead in his family were buried, including three of his dogs. His living dog, Betty, an Australian shepherd, was bouncing around us ecstatically.

"And Betty's going right here," he said, pointing to the tree under which Betty's mom was facing eternity.

"Shh," I said, pointing to Betty, whose ears were both up and alert as she herded the daisies.

"Betty?" said Mack. "Ah, she don't know nothin'."

"*She Don't Know Nothin*", I mused, re-re-revising my epitaph. Or was it better to say: "She Didn't Know Nothin"? Or: "By the Time She Knew Somethin, It Was Too Late"? It's the ultimate writing assignment.

"What's wrong?" he asked me. "Why ain'tcha talkin'?"

"I'm wondering what to put on my tombstone. What are you going to put?"

"Thanks for a Great Time," he said.

Once, before Harry got rid of his prostate cancer, my boyfriend, the one who liked Henry Miller, had asked me, in all seriousness: "What *is* it exactly about your dad having cancer that upsets you so much?"

Shall we pause a moment to parse that sentence in hopes of understanding its meaning? Note the italicized *is*. Note the adverb *exactly*. Note Mack pointing out his from his horse exactly where they'd buried his own dad a year ago.

"Sometimes I wish he was back here beatin' me up again," he said.

Note the clarity in *that* crystalline sentence, the ability of the man who'd not been to college to wrap both arms around contradiction.

The only reason I slept with him was that my mother and I had a fight about flashlights. After their power went out in a rainstorm, I'd bought two flashlights, one to put beside each of their beds. My mother yelled at me for spending the money.

"I have no need of flashlights," she said.

Maybe it was the way she phrased it. Maybe it was my baby picture hanging over her bed, the one where I looked like Harry S. Truman, destined to be single forever, buying things for which no one had need. Maybe it was just the word *need*. Whatever it was, I hurled the flashlight into a wall and then stomped, like a teenager, out of the house. I went down the road, took a right at the goats, a left at the gate, and found Mack disinfecting the head of a mule who'd walked right into a wall of her own.

"My mother hates me," I told him.

"No, she don't," he said.

"Yeah, she do. I threw a flashlight at her."

He put a hand on my shoulder. "Good girl," he said.

I still wasn't attracted to him, and when I saw the tattoos on his aqueduct biceps, I was even less attracted than ever, but since compulsion follows rules of its own, this did not interfere with the sex. The sex—I'm too old to talk about it. Suffice it to say that as soon as we "had" it, or indeed "it" had us, he was the cutest, sweetest man in the world, my first taste of chocolate after aeons of carob, my first golden light after decades of darkness with educated men who knew nothing from nothing.

I signed off as my parents' unqualified caregiver and signed on as their unqualified caregiver slut. The hair shirt flew off, and on flew the sundress, perfume, and mascara. I was a high school crone, sneaking my boyfriend into my bedroom when my parents weren't looking, and for once I thanked God they were virtually deaf. Did I worry that they'd fall on their heads while I was out with Mack on a big bale of hay? I did not. I worried I'd fall on *my* head and meet the big D before I was ready. Now that I had a real man to grow old with, I hoped I'd never be ready. Unless he, too, was ready, at which point I wanted us to slip under twin tombstones next to all his dead dogs. I was utterly overtaken by tenderness for him. You know what I mean: I wanted to see all his baby pictures and suck all the poison from his turquoise tattoos. I even stopped revising my epitaph.

If you're looking for a happy ending, read Sara Davidson's novel *Cowboy*. I happened to, later, and I just about puked because its epilogue (it was more of a rearranged memoir than novel) said that five years later they—the writer and the cowboy with nothing in common—were still together and happy.

But I have an epilogue, too: Five years later, after my *dad* got his turn at crashing (and this time totaling) the car, I moved them into a retirement home and returned to my own "home" back in the city. Mack and I kept seeing each other, but since I was in love and he, well, wasn't, it began to be more torture than fun. Which might be fine when you're stupid and young but is arduous work for a bona fide crone.

My parents like where they're living. Their meals are prepared for them, my mom still has no appetite, and I cross the bay to have lunch with them at least every Sunday. Sometimes Mack joins us and then takes my father to Target.

It's not that he found somebody "better" (well, probably it is, and I just don't know it), but that, despite his seeming invincibility, even he can't stand getting his life smashed again. But isn't that what they all say when, in the horrible parlance of that odious book, they're "just not that *into* you"?

I hate that expression. I hate horses, too, now, every last one of them, plus all mules and goats and chickens with beaks, but I can say without flinching that I do still love Mack. So what if we have nothing in common? I don't think I even know what that means; all I know is that, even now, just seeing him makes me feel grateful and new. As for my epitaph, I'm no longer revising it; I'm not even getting a tombstone. I'm going for cremation, first chance I get, and my urn's not going to say a damn thing.

MY LAST TWO-NIGHT STAND

Laura Fraser

I sat in the passenger seat of a Volvo with a woman I had known for only a half hour, who was giving me a ride home from a party. We chatted. A calm, dark-haired, and pretty woman, Lindy (I'll call her) was a single mother with a serious job. Like me, she was divorced, smart, and over forty—bruised by relationships but still willing to get back into the ring.

We'd been introduced that evening at the birthday party of a guy I'd dated briefly, a never-married man in his late forties who told me, after we'd gotten too close too quickly, that he just wanted to be friends. He's a charming, cheerful, accomplished, and intelligent man, and I have to admit that some part of me clung to the thought that eventually the best relationships can develop out of friendships. So I was an optimist, and a sport, and went to his party.

Over the course of the evening, where Geoff (let's call him) neither introduced me to his friends nor spoke much to me, I became uncomfortable. Making innocuous small talk with the other attractive single women in their early forties who were there—"So how do you know Geoff?"—it dawned on me that he'd once dated almost all of them and then told them he didn't want to be in a relationship. Apparently, he thought such a gathering of "friends" was normal and wouldn't bother anyone. More amaz-ingly, we all showed up.

After I drained my drink and asked directions to the BART train back to San Francisco, Lindy offered me a ride. When we got up together to say our good-byes to the birthday boy, Geoff seemed alarmed. "You're riding home together?"

"Perfect," I said, blowing him a kiss.

On the way over the Bay Bridge I asked Lindy how she knew Geoff. It was the same story: they'd dated, but when he told her he wasn't interested in a relationship, she stopped seeing him. She has a young son, and she wasn't fooling around.

The same thing happened to me, I told her, and to other women I met at the party. I met him, I fell for him—we had so much in common and had such a good time together—and it seemed he fell for me, too. Finally, a real romance. It wasn't until the morning after we'd had sex, just moments after he dropped the condom in the wastebasket, that he mentioned that he ought to make a "full disclosure." It wasn't that he had a girlfriend, he told me, but there were other "situations." And he didn't think he wanted a relationship. Not that he was going to close the door to the possibility. He left me that hope.

Lindy and I started comparing notes: we were both dating him at the same time. He hadn't even hinted to her that he was seeing anyone else. "I was a 'situation'?" she said, staring down at her lap, shaking her head. "That was a situation?"

Well, I told her, apparently I was just nothing at all.

When we realized that he had gone from spending Christmas Eve in her bed to arriving at my house for Christmas brunch, present in hand, neither of us could speak. "I feel sick to my stom-ach," she finally said. I was more outraged, shaking at the memory of how close I'd felt to him that day, almost familial, tak-ing a hike with my best friend visiting from Europe, making a wonderful meal together, basking in the glow of wine and good company. He didn't spend the night. "I have to go see my mother," he'd said.

Lindy, stopping at my house, put a hand on my shoulder. "You know, I think you're great," she said. "And I'm sorry to meet you under these circumstances."

"Likewise," I said. "I'm sorry, too. At least you can say he has great taste in women."

The thing about Geoff, I told her, is that he epitomizes everything wrong with all the men I've been dating since my divorce in my late thirties. He's full of wonderful qualities—he speaks foreign languages, loves the outdoors, and is a great cook; he's funny and unpretentious and bright; he opens doors and pays for meals and compliments you on your shoes. He's handsome—and he knows it. He talks about trips you might take together to South America and makes you start thinking how nice it would be to arrive home from a vacation and drop your bags on the same doorstep.

I've fallen for a string of such men—wildly interesting commitment phobes and narcissists—consistently blind to all the bright red flags waving between the appetizer and the dessert course, carelessly calling for an after-dinner drink. Each time, I ignore warning signs—at forty-six, never married—and my own gut, which tells me I don't know him well enough, he doesn't seem crazy about me, let me wait a few dates and see how he treats me. I focus instead on all his great qualities—his sense of humor, his bright blue eyes, his tastes in music and books that are exactly like mine. I ignore the little voice of my shrink, too, who keeps telling me that the only qualities I should really be interested in are not whether a man skis, speaks fluent Italian, and knows good wines, but whether he adores me and treats me like I'm the most special person in the world. "For such a smart woman, you sure are stupid about men," she has told me.

"We must have the same shrink," said Lindy.

I was puzzled: how could a woman who seemed as together

as Lindy fall for men who don't recognize what an obviously wonderful catch she is?

How, indeed.

It's not as if I've ever set out to have a short-term fling with a man. My hopes for a long-term relationship spring eternal. I meet someone interesting, and I get swept away; it doesn't help that I've had too many drinks and it's been too long since I had my last closely held orgasm. I start fantasizing that I've finally found my new boyfriend—hell, my new husband. Too eager for intimacy, I jump into situations too soon and discover what I already know, that intimacy and sex are hardly synonymous for men. I feel hurt, I get mad, and while there are a lot of confused and creepy men out there, I know I ultimately have only myself to blame. As Geoff said, it takes two to tango, and he understands "no." The whole process is demeaning—and corrosive.

We women in our forties think we're so tough. In many ways, we have to be. We've walked in on our first husbands in the arms of another woman. We've survived divorces and humiliating blind dates and been rejected by men our own age for being too old. We get our hopes up over and over again, only to have them dashed by yet another seemingly perfect man who doesn't want to get involved.

But what I realized that night with Lindy was that I am not tough. At forty-four, I am the most vulnerable I have been in my life. I've been hurt one too many times, I've been alone for too many years, and now I need someone I can rely on. I'm scared of having no one who can help support me as I get older—emotionally, physically, financially—and I'm sad that I have no one on whom I can shower all my love, cheer, and fabulous Italian meals.

When I was in my twenties, I could bounce back from a one-night stand or brief fling (come to think of it, I've never been able to take casual sex casually). But now, each encounter seems like a failed relationship, emblematic of all my failed relationships. Each time, I ask myself what's wrong with me, and the list seems to keep growing. In no other part of my life, at this age, do I feel so deficient. But it seems the more assured I feel as an older woman in the world, the harder it is to connect with a man.

I've had enough. I'm old enough not to be so stupid. I need to learn to value myself the same way I love and admire and support my dear friends. I know what I want: someone to hold me and love me, to intertwine his fingers with mine, to tell me I'm beautiful and kiss me on the cheeks and the nose, the happiest man alive, before getting up to make us both coffee. At this age, I need to be smart enough not to settle for less. A vibrator is a lot better company in the morning than a womanizer.

Lindy and I sat in the car quietly for a few minutes. "I don't think I'm going to see Geoff for a long time," she said. I was actually still debating whether I should take him out for his birthday dinner, as planned, the next night. I didn't want to spoil his birthday. When I said that thought aloud, we both started laughing.

I wish I could say I simply stopped seeing and thinking about Geoff. But when I got out of the car, I went straight for the cell phone and reached him, still at his party. I told him what Lindy and I had discovered: "Christmas Eve in her bed and breakfast with me?" Outraged, I told him how we'd both felt sick to our stomachs, and suggested that he ought to grow up and stop hurting a lot of fine women in their forties.

I lost it; I got angry. I could've saved my breath and energy, because he's not going to change. But at least that anger created an irrevocable split between us and made him finally go away after I'd tried too many times not to see him. When I set the phone down, I vowed it would be the last time I'd go through that wear and tear on my psyche, the last time I'd allow a man to treat me with less than the love and respect I deserve.

I may never see Lindy again, but I hope she spends next Christmas with someone who cherishes her and treats her well. I know I will, even if I spend the holidays alone, with my friends.

THE EX FILES

Jane Ganahl

It's seven in the morning when I get back to my hotel room and crawl, fully clothed, into the unused bed. I doubt I can sleep, but I need to decide how to handle a romantic *situation*, and that's best done under the covers, TV on for white noise and a faux sense of hominess.

It had gone pretty well, this relapse with L, my Most Favored Ex. Maybe a little awkward at first, but considering it had been six months since we'd had sex, it was pretty good. Pretty great, actually.

Pulling the poly-cotton bedspread to my chin as I sink further into the cheap mattress, I feel pleased and slightly schoolgirlish as I replay the evening, still fresh in my mind. We agreed to meet in this town, where neither of us lives, lending the visit a clandestine edge. He was going to be here doing a show, and I was to be on my way home from a work trip. We made a plan for me to find him after the curtain. I got my own hotel room because I didn't know where the night would lead. And because, I reasoned, even if we ended up in bed, I'd need my own place for retreat.

It's a cardinal rule when seeing an ex—even a most favored one: always have an out in case emotions run too high, or you find out he's getting married, or if things just generally get weird.

So I found him as planned after the show: he smiled broadly when he spied me across the lobby. We retreated to the soon-to-close hotel bar, drank a bottle of cabernet and then some, laughed and caught up for hours. He asked me to stay, rather than the other way around. He held my hand affectionately for a while before lunging at me like a bull at a red cape.

Lying here, my body aches deliciously from the heedless way he has treated it during our fifteen or so encounters these last five years. And there had been the sweet good-bye scene an hour ago: I was balanced in my affection and disconnection, and I had not asked the dreaded "When will I see you next?" question. He had leapt out of bed to walk me to the door and kissed me tenderly.

It was, in a word, perfect.

But now, there's the matter of the earrings.

L kisses so hard it's like biting. When he goes for the earlobes, the combination of teeth and metal can be painful for all involved. So I took them out at 2 a.m., woozy from lust and wine, and put them on the bedside table of his hotel (decidedly more upscale than mine).

And there they remain at this very moment, casualties of my night of naughtiness, forgotten in my quiet scramble to collect my things and re-robe before L woke up and saw my naked body—something I'm not too proud of these days. (I know, I know. I should hold my head high as the years smite me with little curve balls like upper arms that are starting to look like tube socks filled with mashed potatoes. And I do, for the most part, as long as there's a robe nearby to cover up my once-pert ass, which travels inches further south every year—much like the San Andreas fault.)

My body is also a reminder to us both than I am, yes, the one woman L has been with these last twenty years who is almost his age. A woman who can empathize with his failings, his moments of brain fade. He forgets to call and check in once in a while; I forget my earrings.

Shit. What to do now?

To ask him to mail them would be asking too much: a presumption that this is a real relationship, which it is not, in which cozy kindnesses are granted. To go back over and get them myself while he's still here in town would seem grasping and needy—almost as though I had planned an excuse for a longer visit—and would ruin the perfect good-bye.

I would write the earrings off, since I have dozens of pairs, but this pair is special—made by hand by my sister-in-law in topaz and amber and silver, and they match a necklace. I really want them back.

This is a *romantic situation,* all right. Not as bad as a *coyote situation,* to rip off that dreadful old male expression. You know the one: a guy wakes up after a one-nighter with a woman he is not at all happy to find sleeping on his arm, and he wants to get away so badly he chews off his own arm to escape, as coyotes have been known to do to get out of traps.

My woman friends have faced the coyote situation in various ways. Sue had a blissful encounter with her Most Favored Ex—someone with whom she no longer desired a relationship but had an itch that needed to be scratched. And, as I'd had with L, they had the perfect night—and the perfect farewell.

She then found that she had left her cell phone in his car.

She bought a new one rather than risk reignition by going over there again. A bit radical, I'll grant you, but some romantic events are meant to be measured in hours, not years or even days. There is potential for bliss, but it's as ephemeral as moth wings. And some exes can be like flames for us: pretty to look at, but Jesus—the damage to your wings!

That's why it's important for an unmarried woman to develop a system for dealing with exes by the time she's my age, especially if she spent a good portion of her life single, and doubly especially if she has gone through periods of tartlike behavior.

Because, face it: by this age, your exes can number in the dozens. Maybe hundreds if you were *really* tartlike.

Some of these exes have faded to memory, and even a Google search won't unearth them again. Others continue to knock on your door, both literally and metaphorically. Some consider you a booty call, which is OK in certain circumstances. But most of my exes are in my life in sweet and natural ways: they ring me for Giants games, advice, recipes.

But there are still those who bear the complications of the last seconds of your relationship: screaming at each other in a parking lot, returning his hibachi by tossing it to clatter at his feet, that sort of thing. The unresolved ones, the ones for whom feelings were nipped in the bud and still lurk like handsome ghosts in your lingerie drawer.

So when the call comes two years later that he's thinking about you and wants to have a drink, be prepared for smart decision making. Should you say yes? And if you do, what is allowable in terms of conduct? A drink? Some sex? Second base while saying good-bye again? It can be complicated.

I know what you're thinking—I think it myself. Why don't I find someone new who is not in the recycling bin of my life? Someone who can actually support and care for me? My eyes are always open for that man, in case he shows up. But at this age, finding a life partner isn't half as important as it used to be. As the years went by after my divorce at forty, damned if I didn't get more and more proficient at being unmarried! You figure out banking, learn how to fix various broken appliances, and you're halfway there. I came to love my personal space more and more, after the initial crushing sadness of Erin's departure for college, and found myself chafing when boyfriends lingered too long in the morning.

I also found myself dating less and less, owing to both my increasing pickiness and decreasing looks.

But it was kind of fine. Waiting for Prince Charming became like waiting for Godot: an exercise in absurdity. Once I realized that he'd lost my number, damn—what a relief! I can have dalliances that are just for fun—just like after my first divorce in the disco era!

Which brings me back to exes. They can make a perfect bridge between the dreadful world of dating and The Future—whether it brings a fabulous man into my life or a seniorhood spent with favored memories.

There are other pluses to getting together with an ex. Attraction is not an issue—unless one of you has grown horns or changed political parties—and you already know each other's likes and dislikes. And when you know you're only getting together for a drink or a dinner or a weekend, there's no need to get bugged about all the things that bugged you when you were an actual couple. These years, I can sleep with L and not even get close to fuming about the fact that he has always preferred twentysomethings to women his age. I don't care, because I don't have to.

(But I mean, twentysomethings. What the fuck is *that* about?)

Yes, yes. On the minus side of seeing exes: the very real potential for pain when emotions reignite only to flame out. Boundaries are challenged, and occasionally a reconnection brings heartache. Or at least shame when you can't resist an ex who doesn't deserve even a slice of you.

One of those e-mailed a year ago and asked me to have a drink. He'd moved to the East Coast and was now married with small children, but unhappy, so unhappy, he wrote. Normally, this ex is one I am more guarded with (he was kind of a dick even when we were dating), but after tales of his faltering marriage and heaps of flattery (show me a middle-aged woman whose self-esteem is perfect and I'll show you a cyborg), we were upstairs in his hotel room, not fornicating but coming darn close.

I got a Christmas card from him later that year, with his lovely wife and two children. Everyone was smiling broadly.

Ick. Shame. Wrong.

I saw another ex recently, the youngest lover I'd ever had, at twenty years my junior. A musician from Texas, he showed up in town recently, and we had breakfast. He reminded me that he had promised to go with me to Paris when I turned fifty; I told him I'd gone two years before without him. He smiled and suggested that he could apologize for missing my big day by giving me a great roll in the hay.

"Darlin'," I told him, taking his hand, "that ship has sailed and so has this body. I don't do young men anymore. It's too much pressure to go to the gym."

Yes, as our middle years encroach, selectivity is key. Not only will I not take any shit in a relationship, I won't sleep with someone who is toned and perfect. Call it a cop-out. I call it Darwinism in action. As my ex-husband, with whom I have never slept again since I walked out the door (which is probably why we're such good friends), likes to remind me: "If you were an Eskimo, they'd have put you out on an ice floe years ago."

And that's just fine. Give me an ex who knows what life is about and has a few laugh lines and some bulges where he ought not.

The best of all worlds, I think to myself, stretching my arms high over the synthetic pillows and emitting a satisfied yawn, is when you have a Most Favored Ex. Someone with whom you have total understanding, great affection, splendid sex, and few complications. Someone who doesn't care that you're not the spring—or perhaps summer—chicken he once knew. Someone like L.

Sure, I admit it took a while to get to this stage of acceptance of what-is. Right after we met, we were so crazy about each other that we called all the time, had bicoastal phone sex. I flew to see him. We even made a stab at a Relationship. But it didn't take long for the rigors of long-distance romance to nip it in the bud: "I can't be a boyfriend right now," he told me sorrowfully, "but I'd like it if we can still see each other from time to time."

I cried some angry tears that first year. His honesty was admirable, and I always like to know exactly where things lie. But I realized I'd finally met someone I could love, and circumstances would not allow it. What's that they say—it's about timing?

Ugh, just thinking of it makes the lump rise in my throat. I'm just tired is all. And last night was really, really great. And it's hard to keep my boundaries intact when it's that great. And I still have to figure out how to get my goddamn earrings back.

It's clear I won't be getting any more sleep this morning. I am too wired and anxious and alive. After a good lay, doesn't one just feel charged with possibility? Might as well get up and take a shower.

My cell phone rings unexpectedly, and I recognize the number as New York. I smile smugly as I purr, "Helloooooo?"

"I'm either going to pierce my ears so I can wear these or sell them for a great deal of money on the black market."

"Oh, did I leave something behind?" I say, feigning a lack of awareness.

"Yes, your earrings, you goof." He chuckles with the deep crackle of a lifelong smoker. "What shall I do with them?"

Ack, pinned like a butterfly in a frame. I had not figured this out yet. *Bring them to me*, I want to blurt out. *Let me come and get them. Let me come and get you.*

"What time are you leaving?" I swallow.

"In an hour," he says, clearly sounding like he's packing.

Bite your tongue, bite your tongue.

"Why don't you leave them with the concierge, and I'll come get them on my way out of town?" I hear myself saying. Who was that? That self-confident woman?

"Good idea. I'll put them in an envelope."

He draws a breath. "It was great to see you."

"You, too. Have a good trip!" Don't say anything else. Just hang up.

And I do. Boundaries intact, one-nighter preserved as perfect.

I wait ninety minutes before I go to his hotel, assuring that I'll miss him. There is an envelope for me at the desk, with my name scrawled in sloppy pen. I look inside, and there are earrings—but no note.

I smile and sigh as I point my car in the direction of home. Sometimes the definition of *perfection* is subject to change.

3.

STRETCHING TOWARD BLISS

Challenging Ourselves to Try New Things

Courage is the price that Life
extracts for granting peace.
—Amelia Earhart

Life is either a daring adventure or nothing at all. Security
is mostly a superstition. It does not exist in nature.
—Helen Keller

STraIGHT outta MarIn

April Sinclair

On the eve of my fortieth birthday, I moved to a small town in rural western Marin County.

"I hope that you're not depending on this place for your social life," said a jovial white male postal worker, greeting my spring arrival.

I shook my head. "Berkeley, Oakland, and San Francisco are all less than an hour away," I reminded him. "I can cross a bridge when I need to."

I could only shudder at the thought of how few romantic prospects awaited a single middle-aged black woman in a town of a little over two thousand. I was one of only four black people residing in Woodacre. The two African American male residents both lived with white women. It didn't take a rocket scientist to do the math. This jolly "Mr. Cholly" who delivered mail could see that I was in the wrong zip code.

Even the professional movers had seemed baffled by my choice to relocate from Oakland to Woodacre. "You have our card, in case this doesn't work out," one of the movers said skeptically. The other added, "I'm sure that we could even work out a discount." I was speechless, torn between expressing confidence and yet afraid to burn my bridges.

What brought me to such a place? The truth is that *Andy Griffith* was one of my favorite TV shows when I was growing up. Like other situation comedies of the time, *The Andy Griffith Show* contained no regular black characters. Yet the show's almost utopian depiction of the charm and innocence of small-town life resonated with me. I was a sista from the South Side of Chicago who had lived in Oakland for fifteen years. But I yearned to find my modern-day Mayberry.

"Are you into white guys or something?" an almost-thirty-year-old woman with long blonde hair blurted out as the two of us soaked in the health club's hot tub. The Women's Fitness Center was in Fairfax, a larger small town, a little over five minutes from Woodacre. I was somewhat taken aback by such a personal question. The fact that we were both completely naked and the question had come out of nowhere didn't help, either. I barely knew this Kara woman. Who did she think she was? But a part of me could understand why someone would wonder why a black woman who didn't have one foot in the grave would move to an area where the pickings were so obviously slim.

I glanced into Kara's blue eyes and shook my head. "I'm not particularly into white guys at all."

Kara sighed and looked at me skeptically. "Then what are you into?" she demanded.

I sighed with a touch of irritation. I thought that since I wasn't into Kara, it was really none of her business. I was trying to come up with a snappy reply, when Kara launched into a further investigation.

"Are you going to Spirit Rock and studying to become a Buddhist nun or something?" she asked inquisitively.

Spirit Rock was a large Buddhist meditation and retreat center situated between the two Woodacre exits. A huge rock on the property could be viewed from the road.

I chuckled. "I've only been to one service at Spirit Rock, and I'm not trying to be judgmental, but I found it boring."

"You didn't like Spirit Rock?" Kara asked with concern. I knew that for a lot of people in the area, Spirit Rock was somewhat sacred, whether they were Buddhist or not. Wasn't everyone around here at least a little bit Buddhist? It was like being into yoga or drinking soy milk.

"I grew up in a black church," I explained. "So I like for folks to make a joyful noise."

"Spirit Rock has a really nice vibe, though," Kara said.

I nodded politely. "I do like Sprit Rock, don't get me wrong. I love to drive past that huge gray rock. And it's in a beautiful natural setting. But when I go to church, I'm not just looking for a nice vibe. I want a spirited sermon and gospel singing. I'm looking for a nice vibe when I smoke a joint."

"Well, Spirit Rock is an awesome place to go and get high," Kara winked.

I smiled. "Funny you should say that. Truth be told, my housemates and I have been up there a couple of times, and one time we got high there. It was truly a spiritual experience," I reminisced. "It's so peaceful up there and quiet and relaxed. All you can hear is the sound of the rushing water from the stream nearby. And seeing the monks tiptoeing around in their robes is so sweet. The only hard part is you have to be quiet, even though you're high and you wanna bust out laughing."

"Yeah, that's when you know it's time to leave."

"Or else go farther into the woods," I continued, remembering the three of us running through the trees, holding our sides in an effort to contain our laughter.

"So, what, white guys just don't do it for you?" Kara asked suddenly.

"They're OK," I sighed. "I just don't have a preference for them. I don't have a *thing* for them. But I'll do what I gotta do.

You know what I mean."

Kara smiled. "That's good, you're not going to shrivel up at least. I was beginning to worry about you."

"Look, I know that my options are limited. But I'm very resourceful. I'm going to do something with somebody at some point. So don't you worry your pretty little head." I smiled as I climbed out of the steamy tub.

I'd recently ended a relationship with a San Franciscan on a very friendly note. We even occasionally still had sex. But I thought the fact that I was a full-time writer who worked at home would make it harder to meet someone new. Luckily, I was a best-selling author. So I went on national book tours, had speaking engagements, and attended literary and social events. On the road, I occasionally received romantic attention from fans, both male and female, mostly in places where I didn't want to live.

I wasn't rich by Marin County standards. That was one reason that I had roommates. The other reason was that I wanted to live in community with other artists. Wasn't I almost living a fairy-tale existence? At least I was until the relentless winter rains compounded my lack of dependable, intimate companionship. And I suddenly began to experience bouts of undiagnosed, and untreated, depression.

But what right did I have I to complain? I was lucky enough to be able to make a living as a writer. I had wonderful, although bridge-challenged, friends. My family was two thousand miles away but close-knit and supportive. I was becoming acquainted with my communicative, artistically talented housemates and several women from the fitness center. What more could I expect?

Not to mention that Woodacre was all so lovely and laid-back. Dogs literally stretched out in the middle of the road. Deer walked around as if they owned the place. And it wasn't unusual to see people riding by on horseback. In fact, there was a ranch down the road that had a stable of horses. So I counted my blessings. I'd chosen to live in an area that allowed me to create while being surrounded by awesome natural beauty. I even had the pleasure of driving through a breathtaking stretch of redwood trees to reach my street. Our backyard was a gardener's paradise, thanks to one of my housemates who'd cultivated it. It was all so charming. But wouldn't my charmed life be even more charming if I had someone special to share it with?

I found myself sitting solo at restaurants and going to movies and to hear music alone, more often than not. Late one night, I left a Fairfax club after listening to a jazz band. I savored the memory of the music as I walked toward my car, which was parked on the town square. Three obviously inebriated people—a woman and two guys—crossed my path. When the three were a short distance from me, the woman turned around and waved a clenched fist into the air and shouted at the top of her lungs, "Black Power! Black Power! Black Power!"

I felt stiff and awkward as her voice rang out in the chilly night air. Surely I was being mocked. But was this racism, or just plain weird? The two guys shushed the woman as if they were either embarrassed or just simply not as drunk as she was. I couldn't tell if they feared what I might say or do, or were actually concerned for my feelings. Maybe they were simply ashamed to be seen with an idiot who was making a spectacle of herself.

Should I have pumped my fist into the air and shouted, "Right on, sista?" And thereby played it off as a joke? But I didn't want the joke to appear to be on me. The only dignified response seemed to be to ignore the woman. Yet I resented the power she had over me to make my hand shake nervously as I fumbled with my keys. Was this woman just a drunken idiot who would regret or even forget what she'd done by morning? Or was she a straight-up racist whose inhibitions had been lowered by alcohol? I comforted myself with the fact that the woman had no visible support for her condescending outburst. Even her friends appeared to be embarrassed by her as they hustled her into the car and sped away.

I sat gripping the steering wheel as I stared into the dark, quiet night. I wasn't even sure how I felt, or how I was supposed to feel. Should I be feeling black rage? A part of me wanted to become invisible. Wasn't that a natural reaction to being thrust into such a glaring spotlight? I'd seen passersby scurrying to their cars as if they also wanted to disappear. How could this be happening in their charming, progressive hamlet? But, ultimately, I was alone in my blackness.

I wished I weren't alone. I believed that if I'd had a man or even a woman at my side, I would've been less of a target. If I'd been with a white person, the outburst probably wouldn't even have occurred. If I'd been with a black man, the woman might've thought twice. Even if I'd been with another black woman, there might've been safety in numbers. Regardless, at least I would've had someone to share the experience with.

I drove silently down the lonely stretch of road, beyond cell phone reception, past the towering White's Hill, and into the tule-fog-covered San Geronimo Valley. I turned left before Spirit Rock and headed through the dark grove of redwood trees. I wished that I had someone to crawl into bed with and hold me that night. But instead I tiptoed quietly into the dark old renovated farmhouse, careful not to wake anyone, and ended up holding myself.

BLUE NOTES

Kim Addonizio

I have developed a little crush on my harmonica teacher. At our lessons, he'll play a tasty blues lick and then sit back on his couch while I make awful sounds on my C Hohner, sounds that always, when I practice at home, bring my cat in to whine and stand on her hind legs and wrap her paws around my shins, begging me to stop. My teacher will nod encouragingly, and then, in his lovely deep voice, he'll begin to talk the obscure numerology of musical scales and modes while I wonder what it would be like to lean over the coffee table, over his roommate's ancient Erector set, and kiss his talented mouth.

Last week he called me about the time of our lesson that afternoon, and the man I live with answered the phone. As the lesson was winding down, my teacher said, "So, that was your husband on the phone today?"

"Sort of," I said.

"How's that work?" he said.

I explained that, technically, I was living with my ex-husband.

Second ex-husband, to be precise.

"I'm a master of the one-minute marriage," I joked. "Sometimes I call him my partner," I said, "but that makes us sound like we're in business together." I realized that I was flirting with my harmonica teacher by trying to sound witty about my current relationship. What is wrong with me? I thought. Then I thought, Well, I'm single. Technically, anyway.

"I could call him my ex," I said, "but that feels wrong, now that we're back together."

Together, but not married.

Not married, but not exactly single.

Tenants in common, according to the deed on the house we bought together two years ago.

What is this obsession with labels, anyway?

It seems to me there is a slippery slope. At one end there is purdah; at the other, the realms of degradation and sluttiness. There are the clearly married, those women who are hermetically sealed into their relationships, like preserves in Mason jars crowded on dusty shelves in dank cellars, never to be opened. And there are the über-single women, most of whom live on TV and are as thin as praying mantises, running around major urban centers in their fetching designer minidresses and disk-compressing high heels. Where does that leave the rest of us?

Think of it this way: in music, a blue note is a "note between" the regular notes of the scale. For example, the flatted third or seventh, according to my teacher, but who's counting?

If I were single, I'd be dating, right? And I don't date. But there is this place between. Sometimes I meet men for drinks. Friends having drinks, what's the problem? So I might say something provocative; so what. So, on a dance floor with one of these friends, I might flash him a tattoo that is in a place on my body that really should be considered private. But look at the world we live in. Nothing is private. Everyone is going around arguing and kissing, or worse, in front of TV and movie cameras. People are peeing in front of Web cams. So big deal.

So, after a few drinks, I might rip the heads off some roses, peel away the petals, and shower them on the head and shoulders of a particularly beautiful man who was in kindergarten around the time I was having my child.

So, at a bachelor party with no stripper, I might feel inspired to get up on the kitchen table, fling off my blouse, and slowly unhook my bra and twirl it around one finger. Hey, I believe in traditions, sort of.

An ex-boyfriend once informed me that I had boundary problems. This is the boyfriend who, when we were together, once took a business trip to Bangkok. "Don't you dare have sex with any bar girls over there," I said to him. I guess it was like saying, "Don't think of an apple." When he came back, he confessed his transgression. I wrote an angry little piece about it, which I labeled fiction, though every word was true. Sometimes, before I gave a reading, he would say, "Oh, read the one about me!"— excited and pleased that he had inspired some of my writing.

I think he had boundary problems, too.

When you become a woman of a certain age—never mind which—life seems too short to take the whole "forsaking all others" thing too seriously, especially when you've already left behind "till death do us part." My husband and I parted for several years before finding ourselves divorced and sharing a mortgage. *Forsake* means renounce, abandon; why would I want to do that to all the lovely men I might encounter? I would rather flirt. I would rather say, "I think I owe you a lick of my lower back tattoo," or, "Why don't you Navy guys at the party towel me off after I jump in the pool in my underwear?" When I meet an ex-boyfriend for dinner (not the bar-girl-buying ex, a different one), I would rather put my arm around his waist and lean in. "I forgot you were so little," he will say. "I forgot you were so big and strong," I'll answer, and then I'll remember how startlingly perfect he looked naked, and I'll get a twinge of mourning for our time together and wish I could step across the boundary of the present to spend just one sun-filled afternoon in my old bed, with him. He'll smell like grapefruit and clean sweat, and I'll be four years younger and infinitely more single, since I'll be living alone and only renting.

So, after our candlelit dinner, I'll do what feels right. I'll give him a hug and then let go. I'll return to my house, where my tenant in common has bought a bunch of white roses and put them in a blue vase beside the bed. He'll be sleeping already, snoring, and I'll give his shoulder a little push so he rolls over onto his side. I'll slip in next to him, and curl around his back, and in my dreams I'll wander through all the houses I used to live in. I'll fly. I'll find myself slow-dancing with my harmonica teacher, listening to a moody tenor sax play a slow, black-snake-crawlin'-in-my-room kind of blues. In the morning I'll wake up and hear the shower running as the man I live with starts his day. Soon he'll leave for work and go into the world, away from me—my partner, my ex, one of my beautiful loves.

FaLLING into ManHOLeS

Wendy Merrill

I had breakfast this morning with my girlfriend Hedy to celebrate my upcoming forty-eighth birthday. We sat in a gazebo restaurant on a beach in Maui, surrounded by palm trees and soft tropical air, and all we could talk about was aging and face-lifts. Hedy qualifies as my plastic surgery expert, having had her eyes and boobs done in her thirties and a full face-lift in her early forties. She's fifty-three now and gearing up for her next round of surgery. After inspecting my face, she said, "If you just get your eyes done now, it's going to look like you've put a brand-new couch on a worn-out carpet. Wait a few more years until the whole face starts to go and have it done all at once." She continued, "You're at the age where it all still looks good, but one day, and one day soon, you are going to look in the mirror and realize that it's all gone to hell."

"Happy birthday to me!" I said, and retreated to my macadamia nut pancakes, wondering if she was right and hoping she was wrong.

It never occurred to me to consider plastic surgery until very recently. I was one of those women who took their looks for granted. I assumed I would somehow be exempt from the aging process, wouldn't care by the time I got there, or would die young.

I was always secretly a bit contemptuous of women who had cosmetic surgery, thinking them vain and insecure. It has since come to my attention that whatever I have contempt for, I should just set a place for it at my table, because it's either already in my life or it's coming.

When I was a teenager, I had contempt for people who drank and used drugs, girls who suffered from eating disorders, and women who lost all their money in connection with "some man." After sixteen years in recovery from alcoholism and bulimia, and having lost all my money in what I call "my spectacular codependent bottom of 2000" with the help of a gambling addict boyfriend, it has dawned on me that I can use my contempt, which is really my fear, to predict my future—or better yet, to change it.

A few months ago I broke up with a younger man—let's call him Brad (since it rhymes with *cad*)—who lives in L.A. and works in the music business. He was another never-been-married-or-had-a-successful-relationship-forty-one-year-old-man-boy-who-lies-about-his-age from Hollywood. In retrospect, this should have been all the information I needed to stay away from him—I wanted a mate, not just a date—but he was sexy as hell and I had been in a penis-free zone for too long.

Thinking that this time it would be different, I used all my powers of denial to ignore the red flags and charge ahead. I figured if I moved fast enough, it wouldn't count as a mistake, like if I eat a chocolate bar fast enough, it won't have any calories. My favorite definition of insanity is doing the same thing over and over yet expecting different results, and this qualified. Not unlike the movie *Groundhog Day*, I seem destined to relive the same relationship, over and over, until I'm willing to change my behavior.

My first moment of clarity came during the holiday season, when I was giving Brad a blow job and realized that I didn't know him well enough to know what to get him for Christmas. I thought this was ironic, but when I told him, he said, "Yes, that is a problem around the holidays, isn't it?" My girlfriends, on the other hand, understood.

My next clue should have been when we were making love and he whispered, "Women your age can't really get pregnant, can they?"

I thought to myself, They shoot assholes, don't they? But I was still having enough "fun" to overlook his comment.

The last time I saw him was when he casually mentioned, "I want to marry someone *exactly* like you, only younger." This is not something that I will ever need to hear more than once, so I said, "Good luck with that," gathered my belongings, and left.

Brad was like an abbreviated version of my love affair with drinking. At first it was fun, then it was fun with problems, and finally just problems. I stopped drinking when I was thirty-one, but I've been falling into manholes since my twenties. At least I don't set up house and furnish it anymore. I was never a serial dater, but I was a serial mater, so after hooking up with the wrong person, I would either marry him or spend years trying to make it work. Now I can fall into and climb out of a manhole in about six weeks, tops (I call this expiration dating), and sometimes even walk around one.

My sister Robin describes my dating history as "Wendy's catch-and-release program," a term used in sport fishing where the sole objective is to catch the critters. I used to think this was funny, until I realized that I was guilty of the very thing that I accuse men of doing. The possibility of a man is more interesting to me than the man himself. If I settle on someone, then the possibility is lost.

When I drank, I chose men who drank more than I did so that they could be identified as the ones in need of help and I didn't have to look at my own behavior. This "thinking" has clearly followed me into sobriety.

The day after walking away from Brad, my ob-gyn called to

tell me that I was in menopause. Men-o-pause. The coincidence wasn't lost on me, but I was startled. How did this happen? What did this mean?

Surprisingly, my first concern was not losing the ability to have children, or getting osteoporosis, but the "sudden onset and appearance of aging." My doctor assured me that I didn't have any symptoms of menopause yet other than irregular periods, and that I was going to age along the same progression that I always have. If I look ten years younger than I am now, in ten years I'm still likely to look ten years younger than I will be. I wonder what forty-seven looks like at fifty-seven.

I was somewhat shocked by my reaction. I had never thought of myself as vain or as someone who needed to have a man around, but then I also never thought of myself as someone who needed to have a drink. Before I got sober, I always told myself that I wasn't an alcoholic—I was just acting like one. Turns out I was wrong, because once I was able to admit that I was powerless over alcohol, my journey in recovery began.

So, is the reality of aging *that* disturbing to me, or am I freaking out about menopause and using the idea of cosmetic surgery to avoid truly being, and seeing, myself? Sometimes it feels as though I'm on a blind date with myself and I'm too shy to look up, or speak. Do I really need to see my beauty reflected in the face of another to feel that I am loved?

My artist friend, Tim, says that the death of an idea for a painting begins with the first brushstroke. By the time the painting is finished, it has become something that may not even resemble the original idea. Having been created, it then becomes a thing on its own, with a life of interpretation independent of the creator. Perhaps my perceptions of men, menopause, and myself are like that, just reflections of the death of my ideas, and now subject only to the interpretation of the observer. The idea that I need a man in my life in order to feel beautiful, the idea of what menopause will mean, and the idea that my value as a woman is dependent upon my looks. I like what Anaïs Nin said: "We don't see the world as it is. We see the world as we are."

So maybe I'll get that eye job, and maybe I won't. But whatever I do, I'll know that beauty lives in the eye of the beholder, and the beholder that matters is me.

Fear of Meeting Mr. Right

Sunny Singh

Call me selfish if you want, but I have to confess that I like my life the way it is. While friends of mine are changing nappies and feeding babies, I can be out on the beach, sipping cold chardonnay. I like being able to pick up my bags and to change countries simply on a whim. And I like not having to plan my vacations with other people's preferences in mind.

Fortunately, it also seems that my biological clock was disconnected at birth. So unlike a lot of my friends, I feel no need to have children. I don't even feel the need to coo over other people's children. Don't get me wrong! I like children, but generally that's linked to liking their parents. So that means that I do babysit for friends and cousins on occasion, but only for the ones that I know have well-brought-up nonmonsters for offspring.

Of course, staying single has not been a conscious decision. Growing up in India meant that one learned about marriages—normally arranged by know-it-all older women—and babies at an early age. But perhaps even back then, my grandmother had an inkling of the kind of granddaughters she had. As a seven-year-old, I remember curling up next to her at one gathering of women who were discussing weddings, suitable boys, and potential matches. "None of these little boys would ever do for my grand-daughters," she had announced, laughing. "I would find those boys crying on my doorstep two days later. My girls are too much for them."

Perhaps somewhere in my mind, the words stuck. And as the years passed, marriage and men just didn't happen. But single-hood did. And for all sorts of reasons. Men I fell in love with didn't want to move around the globe. Men I wanted to share my life with had *their* lives bound to jobs and flashy cars and dreams of home ownership. Which meant that when I got itchy feet, I left them to move to another end of the world. Or they decided that I didn't fit the image of the loving wife and mother. This means, of course, that through the years, I happened to develop a lifestyle that I like and enjoy. And if it happens to be solo, well, that's the way it is.

There have, of course, been moments of anxiety, even doubt, generally thanks to assumptions that women cannot possibly be happy on their own. But over the years, I have realized that being single and Indian is perhaps easier than being single in the West. After all, I was never expected to "find" a man, since that office is traditionally performed by responsible elders. Which took pressure off dating or even "meeting" men. Once I reached my marriage "expiry" date at the ripe old age of thirty, no one bothered about my solo status anymore. And fortunately, no one *ever* expects you to bring a date to an Indian wedding.

In fact, the older I get, the more glamorous my single status becomes. Now I get to advise naive twentysomethings on honey-moon destinations; I help them choose naughty lingerie off the Net and even pass on *Cosmo*-gleaned sex tips to new brides. In the years to come, I have a high chance of growing into the sexiest, most notorious "aunty-ji" on the block.

So it all sounds fine, right?

I thought so! Then, last year, my brother asked me why I

insisted on dating the "wrong" men. I laughed off the question, but later I kept thinking about it.

It is true that I date the "wrong" men. I am very good at dating the wrong men! There have been charming alcoholics, out-of-work actors, embittered painters, and a seriously buff ski instructor. I have told myself initially that I do so because they are more fun than the stable, "eligible" types. We go to all-night raves in the middle of the week and hang out on the beach on Tuesday afternoons when everyone else is at work. Most importantly, they don't last in my life for more than two weeks.

That means that they don't intrude on the life I have created around me. My bedside tables don't need to make space for their stuff. I don't need to move around my clothes to fit theirs in my closet. And I can piss off for a weekend to Amsterdam without wondering about their plans. OK, I admit, it sounds more selfish than usual! But it's comfortable, and safe, and some sophomoric part of me likes adding a notch to that metaphoric belt after I pull some new guy. Besides, I have found that the older I get, the more attractive I am to men . . . and increasingly so to younger men. So it works fine all around, right?

Well, not quite. A few months ago I met a man who seemed perfectly suited to my scheme of things. He was sexy, funny, smart, and an amazing lover. But most importantly (in my opinion), he lived in a different country. So we had a wonderful time and exchanged e-mails, and I put another notch on the belt. There was, I confess, a fleeting moment of regret when I wished that he could have stayed longer. But it passed, and I moved on.

Until he wrote! A short e-mail, but beautifully composed with words like *serendipity* (I know it's sad, but it's one of my favorite words). So I wrote back, and before I knew it, we were setting up another rendezvous. Contrary to my expectations, the next time was even better than the first.

Then we started e-mailing and phoning each other every few

days. And we began planning the next tryst. Before I realized it, he knew more things about me than most people. Not just silly things like my dog's age, but also intimate bits like what upsets or worries me. If I sent an e-mail that seemed distracted, or even terse, he would call immediately to check on me, to tell me that he wished he could be close enough to give me a hug.

Then a month ago, my flatmate left me a note: "Your boyfriend called!" Not a name, not any silly moniker we apply to casual shags. Boyfriend! Worse still, I knew exactly whom she meant.

So now I apparently have a boyfriend. And weirdly enough, my corkboard actually has his photograph. I can't remember putting up a man's photograph in my personal space, unless you count George Michael when he was still part of Wham! And that doesn't really qualify because I was a teenager, and there was never any exchange of conversation or bodily fluids.

But it gets worse. We are off on a holiday together next week, to a country we don't know, and where we know nobody else. I know the place has wonderful weather and loads of things to see and do. He has already told me that he is looking forward to seeing me, to spending time together. A big part of me feels the same way.

However, for the past week, I haven't been able to keep down any solids. I have been surviving on salted cashew nuts and diet cola, since my stomach is in a determined knot. I feel constantly on the edge of throwing up and have had migraines for the first time in my life. I haven't felt so nervous since taking the O-level exams—upon which my college career depended.

It worries me that for the first time in my life I am doing things not at my own whim. That I am traveling to a country that has never been on my list of places to go or see, only because he is there. Worst of all, I am excited about the trip just because I *know* he will be there.

I know I am supremely stressed. And I know this has to do with the man that everyone calls my boyfriend. I am afraid that things will go horribly wrong on our vacation. That we will hate each other, that there will none of the sexual chemistry that has been crackling between us since the moment we met, that we will have nothing to say to each other. But I am also afraid that things will go wonderfully well. In fact, in my more rational moments, I am almost sure that they will.

And that scares me more. He already has a space on my cork-board. Where else in my life will he take up space? It terrifies me that I have met a man whom I don't mind ceding closet space to. Most of all, it worries me that I feel like a sixteen-year-old (thankfully with better fashion sense), with my stomach in a knot, just because of some man.

My flatmate says that I suffer from a fear of meeting Mr. Right, mostly because it would mess up my life that is lived around my own whims and fancies. That I am scared to let someone upset the life I have spent most of adulthood building.

She may be right!

I have spent two decades creating a life far removed from the suburbia-based, BMW-driving, 9-to-5-job-with-annual-career-appraisals lifestyle that most of my college friends have built. In the past two decades, I have accumulated little except for books, which are all stored in my parents' house. My most expensive possession is the computer I use for writing. I have no savings to speak of, mostly because all the money I make goes into traveling. I won't buy designer gear, and I don't own a watch.

In the end, that is what I am afraid to give up. I have seen the alternative, after all.

Over the years, I have seen friends fall by the wayside. Of course, *everyone* is getting married and having babies, which I suppose is a logical consequence of growing up and growing old. Back in India, people I knew from grade school got hitched and pregnant so long ago that now I regularly help their children prepare college applications.

However, something more sinister has happened to my non-Indian friends. On both sides of the Atlantic! Friends who were radicals out to change the world back in college have disappeared.

I remember just ten years ago we campaigned for improving educational opportunities for young people in South America. And my friends from America, the Netherlands, and Spain were all on the same side of the political divide. When we pushed for better conditions for illegal aliens in Europe, we stood shoulder to shoulder, on the side of humanity, not passports.

Then after college, they started working as lawyers and bankers and slowly rose up the career ladder. They found Messrs. Right and moved to the suburbs. And somewhere along the way, they also crossed the line to the status quo.

Now my progressive, intelligent (and mostly white) friends are not only married with children, they have also turned conservative. They wear shoes called Jimmy Choo (when did people start naming shoes?) and drive Mercedes station wagons. And they own more things than can possibly be used in a lifetime. Worse still, they talk of things that were unimaginable in their single days. Now they don't want their children in the same schools as "Arabs," because "their" values are "different."

Friends from Canada, the United States, and Europe who returned to their home countries after years of living around the world now complain of "immigrants." Of course, they don't classify themselves as immigrants, since they were only abroad as "expats." Yet these are the same people who complain about the number of work permits being granted to "foreigners." They don't want to send their children to public schools because of the "mixes." At a recent dinner conversation, one old friend (polyglot herself) insisted that she needed her child to be in a school where he could learn "proper English" first, and not Spanish, Arabic, Urdu, or even Russian.

This is what worries me most. These were people like me once upon a time . . . open to the world and its wonders, with ideals of an equal, rich, diverse planet. They were not scared of differences and changes, and definitely not tied down to a whole lot of domestic machines. Until, of course, they met a Mr. Right.

So this is my question: what if this man who makes my stomach knot up is *my* Mr. Right? What if this begins my slide into the same dreadful, stable, prosperous suburban narrow-mindedness?

Airborne

Judy Blunt

The airport is tiny, one landing strip scratched across a flat spot near Stevi in western Montana. I survive the dive stretched on a blanket outside a prefab shack that serves as the airport's office, squinting up at the sky. Try as I might, I can't lose the mountains. Even lying flat on my back staring straight up, the picture is trimmed in shadow, edged in rickrack. I feel crowded and exposed at the same time, clouds on all sides tacked to a ceiling of unholy blue, the air hanging still, crinkled along the bottom like a drape cut too long. It's the heat that does that, shimmering up. I shift against the hard-packed earth, and moisten my lips. We're just getting started. This is skydiving, a birthday gift to my son Jason. He's a newly minted eighteen. I'm pushing forty-five, middle-aged, tracking the airplane by ear as it climbs. I find the drone comforting in a way, dim at the outside of its circle, coming back higher, and again. And again. As predictable as a pulse. Fifteen minutes, thirty, forty-five.

It's the absence of sound that I wait for, a pause when the engines cut and my son will rise from his crouch, arms crossed over his chest, and arch his head back—a position we called "fully engaged" when he assumed it at birth, some eighteen years and two hundred pounds ago. During the hour-long training session we've learned what to expect, some of it surprising. For instance, despite the name, there's no jumping or diving to this, no self-determination beyond readiness. It's all a matter of letting go: straighten the legs, cross the arms, arch. In that instant, the wind will flick him backward off the wheel strut nine thousand feet above me. For my part, I will wait for that silence, then reach out with both hands and grab the grass on either side of the blanket. Bearing down. Bearing up. Just different ways of letting something happen.

"Would you do it?" he asks me on the drive to the Stevi air field. Jason springs from a cowboy ethic that's hard to replicate in urban life, the sort of "man's gotta do what a man's gotta do" mandate that's a good century out of style. At least that's what I blame for all his posturing this summer: mornings with his friends climbing railroad bridges and leaping blind into the Blackfoot River, afternoons building fences, taping blisters against the shift of a crowbar, bloody nights in the boxing ring. For a moment I'm not sure he's serious. I shift my eyes from the road. As a single parent of three teenagers, I've long since forfeited any pretense of wisdom. I tell him I don't know. Honest, as usual, and vague. I don't know. Or maybe I do. Freefall, 120 miles per hour toward something as flat and hard as I know this world to be? *Too late for me, son. You have to trust the chute.* But I think about it as we barrel down the Eastside Highway.

Like most women reared in the 1950s and '60s, I joined the ranks of single moms without much information to go on. We knew our girls could be taught to take power, but how should we teach the boys? Could we make them surrender what was theirs by birthright? What about the strong male role models everyone said they needed—could we be that, too, or were our sons doomed? I smile to myself, recalling a neighbor mom's compromise; she said she'd given up trying to change her son's behavior and was working on adjusting his attitude. I've not yet given up, but at eighteen, Jason seems slow to outgrow what I call his "Western male death wish" on his own. Most of the men I know applaud some version of their own, I think gloomily. It's hard to know what to do, hard to know if what I'm doing is enough.

His older sister I drag along shopping for cars. I push her hands in dirt. I work construction, sanding and finishing hardwood floors, and I show her the fine edge of tools I've learned to use. Power tools. These things have always been his for the taking. Her birthrights are limitations. She's small, pretty, assertive. She watches the dark corners of parking lots, checks through the curtain before she opens the door. Caution is a form of self-determination for women, a strength, and like most of us, she will generate her own power every day for the rest of her life. Her brother assumes his, like payment due.

Maybe that's why I'm so eager to boot him out of an airplane, I think as the engine grows dim overhead, maybe take a little starch out of him. Fear would be nice, but I'll settle for simple recognition. I want him to see the size of the earth, feel the weight of his own body falling toward it, and know the clear, absolute fragility of both. He might feel his bones shrink to fit a sparrow's skin. He might hold out his arms and fill the sky. It could go either way, I think. Either way.

Clouds drift over the sun, cooling the air instantly, and as I draw in a breath, the engine cuts. The moment he bails is like the moment of conception, almost nothing, a second of silence as the sweat dries and the mind begins to wander elsewhere. I sense the speck of him long before he's visible. Then he's a whisper of buckshot aiming straight for my chest. Then a bullet. With all my strength I do not close my eyes. Of course he is not alone. On this entry into the world, he's tended by men, one experienced diver strapped to his back, two more who follow him from the plane. Freefall is only forty-five seconds. In the training session, we were warned it would seem longer, and it does. Transition, by comparison, is rapid—

against the clouds the first chute opens like a spark in a bale of cotton, then another wink, and another. My gut pulls a sympathetic tumble as we all slow to a float.

I turn loose of the grass and practice my breathing, reentering the scene around me with a start. There's a murmur of voices at a picnic table a few yards away, the woman who runs the office and the wives of the other jumpers having iced tea as they wait. There's the buzz of the drop plane approaching the runway to land. And overhead, three chutes I can lose in the second it takes to blink. Suddenly through a mile of air comes the sound of one boy in celebration, a long Rebel yell *wahoo*-ing faint circles overhead, notes like feathers caught in an updraft. I grin to myself. Apparently he's not scared. The deck is abruptly silent.

"Good heavens," the woman in charge exclaims, her eyes narrowed with suspicion, "is he screaming?" She cranes her neck from the lounge chair, disapproval running a straight line from eyebrow to pursed lip. Just that fast, I'm ready to fight. "Of course not," I snap. Unconvinced, they all shade their eyes and squint upward, conversation at a standstill until they get this figured out. I try willing him to do it again, so they will understand, but there is only one yell and it beats him to the ground by ten minutes.

The men drift, twist, swing in wide loops, the bulk of them growing larger every pass, then one at a time they face the airfield for the final approach. Jason's landing gear is knee to heel longer than the coach's, so he touches down first, legs flexed for a few running steps. The chute hangs high, tugging at his shoulders, then falls in a rush, a huge magenta spray across the grass. The man takes charge of the cords, freeing himself from the boy as I approach. The coach shakes my son's hand, slaps him on the back. Jason can't quit smiling. He can't quit trembling, his lips, his jaw, his hands. Everything shakes. Everything grins. "Great jump," the coach says. "You did great!" Jason nods and laughs, locks his knees and crosses his arms, gathering himself together as the man turns to gather the chute.

On the drive home, my son is all over himself, adjusting his cap, pulling at his sleeves, fiddling with his seat belt. He tells me about stepping onto the strut and looking out over the curve of the earth, how he grabbed the doorframe as he got into position and then could not make himself turn loose. The coach didn't hesitate. He reached forward to cup the boy's hand, prying his fingers free in one twist, and just like that they were airborne. We both chew on this for a minute. When I give Jason back his question, he's still talking in blows and bursts. "Would you do it again?" I ask.

"Whew, man," he says. "Hell yeah, sure. Maybe."

"Whew. I don't know."

NOTHING like Harold and Maude

Spike Gillespie

I was lying in bed one morning, looking around at the posters and paintings on my walls, beloved souvenirs of my past lives. I was in a good space, not taxed by too much work, not in one of my depressions, not sleep-deprived. My brain, forever searching for something to worry about, could not let this placid moment be, and quickly settled on starting an argument with an imaginary boyfriend.

"*No*," I told him insistently, "you are *not* moving in. Things are good the way they are, it's taken forever for me to get to this place, and I'm not moving any of my shit around to make room for yours. I don't need a man in my house or my life, for that matter."

I'd probably been single—not merely partner-free but free of dating, too—for a good four or five years at that point. And single is how I've spent the vast majority of my adult life. The longest relationship I ever had weighed in at about four years. That was with my son's father, to whom I was never married and who left for good when the kid was two.

Beyond that, I had a couple of relationships—including a short-lived disaster of a marriage—that ranged from two months to a year. The rest fall into that miscellaneous category: *one night/ one week/fuck buddy*.

Single, I can now say with the authority of over twenty years of evidence, seems to be my lot. And single suits me fine. I do remember moments of deep, aching loneliness, but those times never lasted long. And if I live the rest of my days alone, I don't think I'll be sorry.

And yet, despite ongoing proclamations advocating the single life, I confess it is entirely possible, at least on one level, that I am protesting too much. Because while I have found a way to be truly content being single, I have never fully eradicated my lifelong desire for a mate. I know this is a mixed message—I love being single, I want a partner—and it is the deepest conflict in my life. But I would rather ponder the puzzle of these two opposing sides of me while sitting alone, deep in thought, than spend my time trying out one man or another hoping for the perfect fit. I've done that too often already, failing every time.

To me, being single used to translate to something negative— I wasn't good enough or thin enough or whatever enough. These days, I'm single in part because I am no longer willing to compromise and put up with the sort of bullshit I put up with for so long to try to prop up one collapsing relationship after another. And therein, I suppose, lies the rub. Compromise, I tell my fourteen-year-old son, is the root of any successful relationship. You have to be willing to give and take. You have to be willing to overlook some things.

I've overlooked enough things. I overlooked that the guy I married forgot to tell me he was a Mormon Republican until after the wedding. I overlooked cheating. I overlooked obesity. I overlooked addiction, unemployment, and possibly covert homosexuality.

I am no longer willing to compromise in what I want from whom I desire. And I'm old enough now to be set enough in my own ways (see aforementioned posters on the wall) that the reality of having to fit some other someone and all of his quirks and needs into my own space seems a rather tall order to fill. (On the flip side, I understand it would be equally unfair to expect someone to put up with, say, my insistence on sleeping with three dogs, my propensity for keeping livestock in the front yard, and my limited housekeeping skills.)

But I do love (some) men. Love, love, love them. And so, in lieu of a real boyfriend, I have come to rely on a string of male companions who have satisfied many, if not all, of my guy needs. In six years there have been six men, each sharing two characteristics: none have been lovers and all have been younger, in some cases, much younger, and a couple of times, much, *much* younger.

I mull causes for being repeatedly drawn to guys young enough to be my nephews. Am I a predator? A Mrs. Robinson? Noncommital? Do I have a need to mother these young men?

The best I can come up with is this: For starters, there just seem to be more young single guys than single guys my age. More importantly, I think I like young guys, especially guys in their twenties, because at heart, I *am* a guy in my twenties. I have no real desire to marry, I don't want (more) kids, I dress in jeans and flannels, I ogle beautiful young women, I enjoy takeout, I decorate my house with interesting pieces of paper I find on the ground, most of my furniture came from the trash, and masturbation is my main sexual outlet.

But there are other reasons I love them. Because these are not interchangeable Lego men whom I nonchalantly replace with ease when one disappears (and they always eventually do). Each has been unique, kind (at least to an extent), and adoring (at least for a while). And, in all but one instance, each has been an improvement over his predecessor.

I recall wanting a boyfriend as early as kindergarten, repeatedly begging my mother (she of unwavering refusal) to allow me to bake a birthday cake for John Logan, my then-crush. A kiss or two from Steve Costello in high school and dry-humping Irish carnies during teen summers at the Jersey Shore notwithstanding, I didn't actually score a "real" boyfriend until I was nineteen and a college sophomore. Because I have already spilled countless gallons of ink and tears describing this man and the dozen or so that followed him, I'm going to set my own world record for succinctness here and say that, at forty-one, I *still* have not located the sort of boyfriend I always really wanted.

I think part of my failure to locate a suitable companion is that, for a very long time, I was too chin deep in my own emotional shit to know what I wanted for myself in life, let alone to be able to understand what I wanted from someone else. But the blessings of time and trauma and therapy and yoga and martial arts and meditation and a dozen pets and sundry other trappings of early middle age have at last opened my eyes. I know now precisely what I want in my other half. I know even better what I do not want. For one thing, he will not be saying stuff like, "Well, you can't call me *boyfriend*," or, "We aren't *monogamous*, OK?"

Those were both favorite and oft-repeated statements of my last boyfriend (oops, I mean, the guy I fucked regularly, learned how to make complicated moussaka for, and was at the beck and call of, although technically he wasn't my *boyfriend*), as if we were in second grade and not our thirties. He really was awful. After him, I said, *That's it, no more, fuck you, fuckers, I'm taking me out of this stupid-ass dating game, your loss, not mine.*

Oh, wait, that's not how it actually happened. How it actually happened is, I cried for, I think, about two years. And I still have recurring nightmares in which he comes back after cheating, much as he did in real life, begging for one more chance. And I hate myself for it, but in these dreams a part of me always wants to take him back.

I don't think this means I miss that guy so much. Admittedly, the sex was balls-to-the-wall (and other interesting positions), but the sheer hell he put me through (or, to use therapy speak: that which I allowed myself to be put through) finally made me understand that all pain does not equal all gain; it equals no gain at all. I think I dream about him for the same reason I sometimes dream I'm smoking or drinking again—so I can wake up and feel relieved that, thank God, I'm not.

That relationship ended in 1999. Jared showed up unexpectedly right afterward, a friend of a friend who made me laugh uncontrollably when I wasn't totally bereft with grief. Jared, the silly joker, the brilliant artist, the delightful oddball, the lover of all sorts of music, a near-constant companion, and, at eight years my junior, younger than my youngest sister, a fact I alternately identified as alarming and a little bit exciting, as I wondered if we might ever date.

But while our brain love was mutual, our physical chemistry was not. When he had a fling with a mutual friend, it was a reminder to me that most guys in their twenties (and maybe thirties and forties and fifties and sixties)—no matter how openminded and sincere and adoring—when given a choice between a very smart, average-looking woman and a hot woman of average intelligence will be tugged by their dicks toward the latter just about every time. (Or maybe I'm wrong. Maybe age kept Jared from being interested. Or maybe if I had been built like a brick shithouse and twenty-five, he still would've turned away. I just recall that, after being so very close for so very long, it hurt so very badly for him to leave me like that.)

Erik, five years my junior, was a self-proclaimed sex nut who bragged regularly of his allegedly huge cock and who, I'm sorry to note, was probably only teasing me with all that sex talk so that I would feed him and slip him the small loans and joints he was always in need of. Our one attempt at coitus was interruptus pre-foreplay, leaving me forever unable to definitively report back on his boasted length and girth (something I would come to be grateful for later).

Bob was six years younger. A gentle overdrinker who could recite poetry on command, he appealed to my inner English major. I drove twelve hours straight to Nebraska to bake him a birthday cake (which I regrettably did not ask my mother's permission to do). Bob was nice about my obvious crush, and when I poured out my longing in a beautiful greeting card (the kind preferred by middle-aged women), I proclaimed love for both his mind and his mortal coil, dreaming the Shakespearean reference might win his heart.

It did not. The last time I called him, a woman's voice answered, sounding first suspicious and then, when I asked if she was his sister, very annoyed. I have not called since.

Shawn was all e-mail, a fact checker on a story I wrote. Another tease. Thirteen years younger. He had a girlfriend and a mean streak. We met once. I gave him a rock; he gave me a banana. "Thanks for the banana," I wrote later. "I really enjoyed it. Then I ate it." That was as close as we got to consummation.

With Ben I got warmer and colder at once. Ben was three weeks old (and I, a high school junior) when I went to my first rock concert. The nephew of my good friend, he and I became intensely close when he moved home after college, awaiting assignment from the Peace Corps. I studied my attraction to Ben. It wasn't lust based, though certainly he is very attractive.

His voice matched the voice of my kid's father, my longest, truest love. Maybe that was it. Or maybe it was some innate bio-urge, out of my control, my aging womb begging for one more chance before the old biological clock slammed shut the window of opportunity to procreate.

Was nature really pointing me to a young fertile stud with whom to reproduce? I remember being on an early-morning hike with Ben in the springtime in West Texas in the Davis Mountains.

We balanced rocks upon rocks and didn't say much, but if I were a latter-day Poe, I could've written on the spot "The Telltale Ovum," for I knew I was ovulating, I could hear it loudly in my ears, and I knew, if this were a movie or a novel, we could, right here on this very spot, conceive a child that would, among other things, infuriate Ben's mother, who was closer to me in age than her son was—by several years.

I didn't say a word to Ben about my feelings. I did, however, joke about my urges in a broad way, noting that turning forty made me feel the need to either have a baby or start raising chickens. Within the week Ben built me a coop, announcing, hammer aloft, "This is my version of Planned Parenthood for you." Ben left for the Peace Corps last year. Two of my chickens are named for him. I send him packages in the jungle—art supplies, candy, music—and he signs his notes, "From your Prince in Belize."

Not long after Ben left, I started to fish around in the supernatural realm, asking the universe what I was supposed to do about this deep conflict I was feeling, being happy on the one hand with being alone and not having to compromise, but feeling some deeper gut pull to find one-on-one love.

Looking toward the spiritual for answers wasn't new to me. A devout Catholic for the first nineteen years of my life, I also acquired my first book of the occult in elementary school. I'm big on signs, whether real or imagined, if for no other reason than to have a focal point as I attempt to resolve issues. For a long time, the daily horoscope sufficed—the ambiguities contained therein suiting my own vague views of what I wanted.

But yoga and meditation, and dipping my toes into Buddhist studies—all of which began strongly appealing to me in the late '90s, as forty loomed—led me to desire more precise answers. What *was* the right way to conduct my life? What *was* it OK to hope for?

My questions led me to the teachings of psychic Sonia Choquette, who has a comforting, peppy style that could lead you to believe thorns are the most preferable parts of roses. Sonia suggests making a wish box into which you place your three greatest desires. As I understood it, this helps you admit things you might be afraid to wish for out loud. It also helps you to focus on them.

I didn't want to be stupid with my wishes. In my life I have been humbled by many things—my abusive father, my addictions, a malignant ovarian tumor, a child who nearly died at birth, a foolish marriage to a dangerous man. I decided to wish carefully in regards to a relationship. Rather than wish for a partner, I asked only for clarity, once and for all: *Do I want a boyfriend or don't I? Is the conflict I feel between single vs. couple real, or is it a residual, pathetic, unrealistic, unfulfillable desire foisted upon me by media messages about princes and happily ever after and true love that can't possibly really exist?*

Not long after, an ex-boyfriend resurfaced. A decade of being apart dulled bad memories of that relationship, and I found myself surprisingly slipping toward re-smittenism. Which is when I did a very naughty thing. I placed his business card in the wish box, convinced the feelings he evoked had offered me not only an affirmative answer to my query (*YES!* cried the Magic 8 Ball. *It is certain! You DO want a boyfriend!*) but went so far as to tell me who that person was.

Of course, this backfired. He didn't call and didn't call and didn't call. But as an item on my very short Wished For list, I focused and focused and focused on him, quickly slipping from re-smitten to re-tortured, envisioning him laughing maniacally each time he walked past his telephone, purposefully not calling me. Some old therapy bubbled up and intervened, thankfully, and before I could get to the part where I started listing all of the things about myself I should change to make him want me, I extracted the card and took a match to it, not in a psychotic fashion, but merely for ceremony.

The card, coated in some sort of plasticky finish, failed to burn but did give off choking fumes.

Still, I had my answer. I *did* want a partner, even if it meant having to give up insisting that I wanted a hairy dog ass on the pillow beside me at night rather than a man. I replaced the wish for clarity with a wish for a strong, fulfilling, monogamous relationship with a mutually loving partner. In addition, also based on the advice of Sonia, I wrote down all the traits I wished for in my idea of the right man. I put this on a separate piece of paper and included things such as:

Loves me
Loves my kid
Doesn't want kids
Loves sex
Plays guitar
Loves music
Isn't an addict
Loves Japan
Loves food
Good-looking
Independent
Monogamous
Funny

Enter Southpaw Jones, the singer-songwriter friend of my singer-songwriter friend Matt the electrician. In March 2004, Matt played a show at which Southpaw also played. Which is how I happened to encounter Southpaw for the first time. There isn't an accurate way to capture how I felt when I first heard Southpaw's songs, because "blown away" is terribly overused. I signed up for his e-mail list, bought a CD, went to another show or two, and then, for whatever reasons (my busy life, Ben's pending departure), Southpaw dropped off my radar.

Until . . . until I put that list in the wish box, the one naming all those good traits. Shortly after, Southpaw played at a show I was emceeing—I had booked him many months prior. As I stood introducing him, I was overwhelmed with some bolt-of-lightning feeling I couldn't explain. It startled me, and I blurted out to the large audience that here was a man I wished were older because I would jump him in a heartbeat.

This was not the first mouthy or surprising thing I ever said into a microphone. Hell, it wasn't even the first time I propositioned someone over a PA system. But those other times I'd been joking, and here, beyond my control, true words poured from my pie hole.

Southpaw took it in stride, at first claiming to be thirty-seven, then admitting that number was ten years too high, then covering his bases by saying, with the audience as our collective witness (even if he was joking), that he thought fourteen years was a good age spread between partners. His humorous grace under my Mrs. Robinson pressure, and a gorgeous performance that night, stuck with me. I sent a long and gushing letter, bold even for me, in which I reemphasized my crush upon his tender young heart and wished for some way for him to time-travel across our chronological chasm and be mine.

Disclaimer: When I sent that letter, I can say with all honesty that I did so from the distant stance of an older woman who knows she's an older woman and recognizes the difference between fantasy and reality. I did not literally proposition him in any way, only wished he'd been around when I was his age.

Maybe, more accurately, I wished that when I was his age—back when my chances of dating were not slimmed by graying hair, and spreading ass, and increasing curmudgeonliness—I had

had the confidence to make sincere and bold statements of love and allegiance to good-hearted and deserving men. Instead, too shy, too insecure, too unclear of what I wanted, all I could do was lube up with two pitchers or three and wind up in the bed of one man or another, all of them terribly wrong. I did not feel allowed to want what I now know I wanted then, the thing I want now, the thing we all want, the most simple and most elusive thing in the world: to be and feel truly, deeply loved, and to share that love with equal depth.

I invited Southpaw for supper, hoping for a friendship. It didn't take too long for us to insinuate ourselves into each other's lives. Like a dog worrying a spot of mange, when I was alone I leaned toward my age-old habit of overanalyzing a situation and picking at my emotions like scabs. But in the presence of 'Paw, these things simply slipped away. And I could see a simple reason why: he would not feed the worry; he came with no fuel to pour upon the fire.

He is simply himself, no secrets, no games. He likes me, makes this clear, hangs out, does not rush to go. He gives me gifts, sings me songs, laughs at my jokes. I think, no matter how old we get, women have a tendency to believe that if they voice their love or desires or hopes, particularly to a man for whom they feel affection, they will be greeted with some variation of the elementary school taunt, "EWWWW, that is DEE-SKUS-TEEEEN."

What makes us think this way? Why couldn't I ever let that fear go? And where, now, so suddenly, has it gone?

I e-mailed Southpaw when it dawned on me. "I wished you into my life," I told him. But there was one thing I forgot to put on that slip of paper. Nowhere on it did I write, "This is the man I want for a boyfriend." I simply described a wonderful human, and that human waltzed into my life.

I dated a man seventeen years older than me once, a very long time ago. Andy remains one of my closest friends. But I could not get past the hurdle of our age difference, pointing out to him he was old enough to have driven me home from the hospital when I was born. (He didn't mind. Later he married a woman much younger than me.) Likewise, despite a fondness for Southpaw that grows regularly and exponentially (if this is possible), I continue to have no unrealistic expectations but hope only that our friendship will be as deep and long-lived as mine and Andy's.

Supernatural me predicts that one day, soon enough, Southpaw will find a girlfriend, a woman his age, whom he will love deeply, who will love him back equally. This doesn't worry me. It's what he deserves. It's what we all deserve. I have my answer now, and I doubt the source will leave me anytime soon, no matter who else shows up in his life.

As for me and my future, I believe my wish box works, but I am in no rush to re-create that slip of paper and stamp *Life Partner* across the top this time. Southpaw and his easy way have, at last, presented me with the long-missing piece of my puzzle. His presence speaks to me, even when he is being his quiet self. *Here is what it feels like*, it says, *to be comfortable with a man, to hang out, to laugh, to not worry, to say exactly what is on your mind.* This is the feeling I always knew was out there, and if I wasn't so glad to find it now, I would weep at how long it has taken to locate. Now that I know it, I stand ready to recognize it when I do decide the time is right to finally put the Big Wish into my box.

4.

GOING IT ALONE

Serene—and Not So Serene—Independence

No matter how lonely you get or how many birth announcements you receive, the trick is not to get frightened. There's nothing wrong with being alone.
—Wendy Wasserstein

Independence is happiness.
—Susan B. Anthony

LOCKED IN

Lynn Freed

A version of this story was published in the *New York Times Magazine*, March 22, 1992.

Some years ago, I decided to move from San Francisco, where I had lived for twenty years, to a small town in the Wine Country, an hour away. A seventeen-year marriage was behind me, my daughter was leaving for college, and I was mad for the idea of a new life. Alone. Signing the papers on the new house, it did not occur to me that I might not be suited to life in the country. I had lived in cities all my life and now I wanted peace, I told myself. Peace, privacy, and safety. At least that was the list I presented to my incredulous friends.

In fact, my quaint Victorian bungalow, surrounded by vineyards and three blocks from the center of town, soon became the darling of my acquaintances. They would arrive from the city, ecstatic with the beauty of the journey—the hills, the vines, the cows, and the sheep. They would sit on my deck under the walnut trees, exclaiming on the charm of the place, how lucky I was, how clever to have moved here. And then, when the sun began to set, they piled into their cars and went home.

Waving one's friends back to the city, I found, wasn't all relief. Peace can be deadly, particularly when it comes in the evening after a day of silence in the studio. But the price of company for an evening was company for the night—the guest room

141

readied, vacuum cleaners got out. Unless one is fiercely protective of writing time, days can be lost this way. And if one *is* fiercely protective, one can die of loneliness.

Still, still there were compensations. I did not need earplugs to sleep. The sun shone in summer. The air was fresh. Every morning, there were birds on the lawn eating things. I had as much privacy as I wanted, and I felt completely safe. I could walk anywhere I wished, day and night, without city vigilance. I could leave my windows and doors open, my keys in the car. The whole arrangement seemed quaint to me. This is the way America was in the 50s, friends told me. This is how they had grown up themselves.

And then, one day, I opened the local paper and read that a rapist had attacked a woman viciously, not half a mile from my house. The woman he attacked was about my age, living alone, on this side of town. Two weeks later, two blocks away, he hit again. The town was in an uproar. Meetings were convened. Psychologists and rape counselors and locksmiths and policemen and sheriffs all had something to say. Women came forward, single women in their forties and fifties, who had this and other things in common with the victims: outdoor lightbulbs unscrewed, windows broken, small items filched from their houses. The story made it into the San Francisco papers. Friends phoned in alarm and, perhaps, a little glee. Come back to the city, they said. Stay with us. And shouldn't you get a dog? A gun?

No, no, no, I said, trying to take comfort in the fact that I had never been a natural target, not even for panhandlers. I walk fast and determined and straight. I look fierce without even meaning to. Still, it was the dangers of the city that I was used to. I knew what to avoid there, and when. A serial rapist who stalked his victim for months before hiding himself in a closet in her house was not a danger I had ever considered before.

Now, however, I saw him in every man I passed. I came to

feel watched myself. And the night took on old childish terrors. So did dark places, and odd sounds. A walnut falling onto the roof had me out of bed and all the lights on. If I came home in the dark, I did not park in my garage. I left my outdoor lights on and checked each day that they were still screwed in. I had a fence built to close off the garden from the street, with a lock and a peephole.

Once peace was shattered, next went privacy, which had been first on my list to the real estate agent who had sold me the house. To someone like me, someone cursed with compulsive politeness to those who are not my intimates, privacy is key to peace of mind. But now it became clear that I had to know my neighbors—not only the set I knew already, but all of them—both sides, behind, and across the road. More than this, they had to know me. They had to have my phone number and to feel free to call if they didn't see a light on, or if they did. We were to meet and consider banding together into a Neighborhood Watch arrangement, which would require monthly get-togethers, like Tupperware parties, at each other's houses.

I attended meetings, wondering whether the friends weren't right, after all: I should go back to the city. Meanwhile, I swapped names and numbers with other women, women with whom I had nothing in common except fear. They phoned to give me the latest information and to invite me to more meetings. I phoned the mayor and demanded to know what was being done to catch the rapist, why experts were not being called in to solve the case. There have always been rapes around here, the mayor told me. Two rapes on the better side of town were not sufficient cause for calling in experts.

When a third woman was raped and savagely beaten two blocks away, I signed up for a self-defense class. Next to me in the class sat a single woman who had had her outdoor lights tampered with, her windows broken. The policeman who had come to investigate didn't report the incidents, she told me, so she had bought a gun. A woman on the other side showed me her new car phone. There were rumors, they told me, that the rapist was a gardener, a construction worker, a policeman himself.

The rapist can be any man, said the Assault Prevention Expert, waving a can of tear gas at us ($37.57). I considered the pharmacist, the mailman, the supermarket bagger, the man whose dog fouled my grass every morning. I had heard that men were afraid now to walk their dogs without their wives at their sides. I had seen men walking down the middle of the street, staying out of shadows. I myself had walked like this. I had wandered the streets of Istanbul, Cairo, Rio, walking in the light. But never until now had I felt that normal caution was useless; that I could have been the victim of Anyman, any man at all.

"Don't be a victim," said the Expert. She handed around a Personal Security Products Catalog. She showed us the Personal Alarm, which had a ghastly shriek ($32.57). Then there was a stun gun that could have a man down on the ground while you ran ($96.70). But I didn't want to run. Suddenly, I wanted to hold the rapist down in agony until he begged for mercy. I wanted him put into prison so that he could be raped himself. I wanted his life diminished, his body too. More than this, I wanted him to know that I was the instrument of his downfall.

When I got home, the house was silent and cold. I locked myself in, as I was now accustomed to do, still enraged. I looked into the closets, under the bed, set the alarm. Then I settled down to admire my arsenal. But, spread out on the kitchen table—fashioned in cheap black plastic, or closed into black vinyl holsters—the devices looked like dime-store junk. Also, I had bought too many. I suddenly realized that one can use them only one at a time. And, anyway, I still did not feel safe.

So, what would it take, I wondered, to feel safe again in the country? If the rapist were caught, would I drive into my garage after dark? Would I leave my front door unlocked, sit out in the sun without my Personal Alarm? In time, perhaps, I thought. In time, in fact, I did. The terror subsided, the urgencies dissolved. Men began to walk in the shadows again; women stopped buying weapons. Even my friends came around again to say how lucky I was to be out in the country. Clichés were invoked: I had taken the bull by the horns, they said, moved out of a marriage, out of a city. Pleased to be envied, I did not tell them that life on one's own might not be all they imagined. The freedom? Yes, but what about the long march alone into old age? Infirmity?

Still weighing the balance, I stay on alone, year after year, a city woman in a country place.

I still walk straight and fierce, tapping real fury at the thought of a stranger with the power to rob me of my peace of mind, and I have come to understand that peace and privacy cannot be bought and sold. That safety is an illusion that begets itself. That women are safe nowhere, and probably never were. Not even in marriage. Not even in the 50s.

one single day

Kathi Kamen Goldmark

I stood in the narrow hallway of a shoddy Chicago high-rise, holding back tears as I handed over the contents of my wallet: all my cash, a supermarket discount membership, nail clipper and comb, and a Visa card, nearly maxed-out anyway, so it didn't matter that much. I tried to bite my lip to keep from speaking my mind to the tall, intense young man who now had all of my portable belongings, but somehow the words came out anyway.

"Take your vitamins and don't eat too much junk, OK? And if you feel lonely, don't sit around moping; go out and do something. Chicago is a great city; maybe you can get a fake ID so you can go to blues clubs. Don't let this place turn into a pigsty; at least throw your food garbage away every day. Remember there's a Freshman Center where they have people trained to help you with problems. That page of phone numbers in your white binder—all friends of mine who said to call if you need anything—Norm at WXRT can get you tickets to most of the cool shows. You just have to ask. . ."

My son rolled his eyes, gave me one last hug, and closed his apartment door. For the first time in his life, he was on his own. For the first time in over twenty years, so was I.

My husband had moved out of our San Francisco house a

few months earlier and we were lurching toward finalizing a messy, ambivalent divorce. Dealing with the mediator and lawyers, gathering information and notarizing papers, I felt as if I had taken on an unpleasant extra part-time job. Feelings were raw, the atmosphere filled with anger and disappointment, with occasional unsettling moments of mutual appreciation. It was weird and sad, but also kind of a relief when he finally moved out. The summer had been a whirlwind of preparing our only son for his first year of college. I had barely noticed the empty closet, the missing pasta pot, the fact that I was still sleeping on "my" side of the bed and turning the TV off before going to sleep, observing obsolete rules of my marriage.

So there I stood in a hallway in Chicago on the first day of the rest of my life. I pulled my plane ticket out of my nearly empty purse and noticed the date: September 20. It would have been my twenty-first wedding anniversary. It was also going to be my first day living alone in more than twenty-two years and, as it happens, it was the publication date of my debut novel. My first bookstore reading was scheduled for 7 p.m., two thousand miles away. There was nothing to do but make sure I got on that plane.

Beyond exhausted from four nonstop days of prefab-furniture assembly and last-minute parenting, I braved the Blue Line and made my flight with time to spare. Curled into my window seat, I tried to make sense of the day and sort out my feelings. I was exhilarated by the grand adventure ahead, lonely and sentimental on the anniversary of my defunct marriage, terrified about finances, sad and guilty over the divorce, thrilled beyond words that my novel had been published—and looking forward to knocking 'em dead on a multicity book tour—but also cynical in the way that only someone who's worked in publishing for many years can be.

I was both proud and worried about my son. He was still reeling from a difficult adolescence and had been proclaimed by three shrinks and two grandmas to be "not ready for college—don't be surprised if he's home in three weeks." I was concerned about the backlog of tasks waiting for me at the office where I worked as a book publicist. I wondered how I would lift the heavy bottles of spring water onto the dispenser in my kitchen and felt shameful delight that I would never again have to look at the yucky old cast-iron hamburger grill that now resided in my ex's beautiful new apartment. I was nervous about my reading later that evening. Have I mentioned that I was thrilled beyond belief to be a published novelist? It was all too much, and I decided—right before dozing off in my cramped little seat—that it would be best for everyone if I just went numb for about a year and didn't feel anything at all.

Being numb worked great that first day. It helped me deal with my pissy boss when I arrived at work later than expected, directly from the San Francisco airport. It helped my heart not stick in my throat whenever the phone rang, thinking the caller might be either a sentimental ex-husband or a certain kid in trouble in Chicago. It even helped me stay relatively calm through my public reading that night. I changed clothes in the bathroom at work (luckily my son had had no need for the makeup in my purse). There was a nice little crowd waiting for me at the bookstore, everyone seemed to have a good time, and a few people I didn't know personally even bought books. My parents were there, as proud as could be, and we went out for dinner afterward; it was a lovely evening—so lovely that I had to keep reminding myself that I had gone numb.

Pulling into the driveway later that night, I noticed one of the dreaded heavy water bottles on my front steps, alongside a pile of newspapers—oops, I'd forgotten to stop the paper—and a vase of flowers, the traditional "pub date" gift from my publisher. I dragged everything inside, closed the front door, and started going through piles of mail, noticing that—yikes—the house was exactly as I'd left it. There was no pile of Weird Al videos on the living room sofa, no dirty towels on the bathroom floor or leftover bachelor-dinner spaghetti in the fridge. The clothes I'd decided not to bring to Chicago were still piled on my unmade bed. It was real—I lived alone.

Those weren't tears smudging the mail as I sorted through scary bills and tossed the junk into the recycling bin. No tears stained the blouses and slacks I crammed into my closet next to clothes I hadn't worn in years—fat clothes and thin clothes, work clothes and dress-up clothes. Certainly there were no tears on the pillow on my side of the bed as I listened to the creepy creaks and squeaks of a too-big-for-one-person house that needed work and tried to sleep. If any moment was ripe for a good cry, this might be it, but I had gone numb, and I was determined to stay numb.

Jarred out of a fitful sleep by the phone, I heard my son's voice on the line sounding far away and a bit shaky, complaining of a pain in his chest and asking where to find the Advil. I told him to look in the medicine cabinet and made him promise he'd stop in at the student health center in the morning if it still hurt. We chatted for a few more minutes until he shyly asked if I would mind singing him a favorite childhood lullaby to help him fall asleep. Voice cracking with gratitude for this gesture, for his willingness to let me know he still might sometimes need a mom, I sang the song all the way through for the first time in many years, and gently hung up the phone. Then, unable to fall back asleep, I began wandering around the house, taking inventory and making a list of things I now needed: a laundry hamper, for example; a teapot; a favorite Johnny Cash CD.

I opened the closet where my husband had kept his clothes, momentarily startled to find it empty. Then I had an idea. Rushing back to my own overstuffed closet, I looked at each item carefully, selecting and removing a few things—nothing too big or too small, nothing unflattering or unfashionable. I stocked my new closet only with clothes that fit perfectly, that made me look good, that I loved to wear. The rest—my beloved old rock-and-roll size 6s (I think they fit for about twenty minutes in the 70s), that favorite big shapeless thing I wore when I was pregnant, the schmatte with the beaded leather fringe, the horrid what-was-I-thinking" purple formal, the nice-ish pantsuit with the safety-pinned hem—all stayed, to be dealt with slowly over time. My new closet would contain only clothing that fit, only clothing that looked good enough to be worn by a published novelist—one who might even, at some point, be willing to share her closet again.

Then I turned on the television, nice and loud, and found a corny old movie. Plunking my pillow down dead center in the middle of the bed, humming my son's favorite childhood lullaby, I tucked myself in.

TWO LIVES

Isadora Alman

Could it be that many years since we last saw each other? New York City, 1960s. The four of us worked together in a government office that frowned on intra-office socializing. Civil Serpents, we called ourselves—Mavis and her new husband, me and the man I eventually married, brought together by their secret marriage, our clandestine courtship, and by the similarities of the couple balance. Mavis and I were outgoing, sociable, politically principled, pre-Lib liberated women. The men were handsome, shy, introspective, let's-leave-well-enough-alone types of their respective (middle) classes. There were differences. My soon-to-be husband and I were New York Jews. Mavis and Mike were midwestern Catholics. Mavis was black. They were several years older at an age when those things could matter. But we were good friends— the two men, the two women, and the two couples.

Ours, however, was the intimacy of that time and place. When Mavis and her husband announced their intention to remain childless, they couched it in terms of the hard life of a racially mixed child, not their obvious disinterest in being parents. They all teased me about the number of cigarettes I smoked, but no one mentioned, even in jest, that Mike almost always had an open beer in hand during nonwork hours. It was observed that my husband-to-be and I often went to his nearby apartment for lunch, and though we were seen to gobble sandwiches on our coffee break, they did not allude to what we might have been doing previously that day rather than lunching.

When Mavis and I were alone, we shook our heads at our men folks' reserve. "Girl, I worked all day to gussy myself up and don't you know that he would choke rather than tell me I looked pretty!" I swore that when the laundry starched my husband's undershorts he wore them without a word. The men laughed about Mavis's false eyelashes and the beauty mark I always painted near my left eye. They insisted that the petitions for a variety of good causes we always seemed to be carrying in our purses were all for Communist front organizations and refused to sign any of them, ever. Such were our secrets and the stuff of our shared intimacy.

Mavis and Mike were the only mutual friends we had made as a couple and the only people from work to attend our wedding. In fact it was Mavis who was instrumental in finding my husband the job that enabled him to quit the civil service and us to marry. Even without the bond of a common workplace, the four of us remained friends. Although my husband and I often remarked in private that we thought them an odd and mismatched pair, we laughed at the certainty that they said the same about us.

My husband and I moved to California. For a while there was an exchange of holiday cards and photographs—their new summer home, our new baby. But for many years, nothing more. Then a phone call on my daughter's phone, the only San Francisco listing with that long-ago married name. When I heard that gleeful shriek and that pseudo-ghetto "Girl? Is that you?" Mavis and New York and other times overwhelmed me with their immediacy. Passing through from somewhere to somewhere else with a few hours between planes, Mavis gave it a try. I was at the airport within the hour.

"You haven't changed at all!"

"You look exactly the same!"

Hugging and jumping up and down, we gushed what everyone wants to hear from old friends. No, she didn't look exactly the same, but almost. Tall, elegantly and flamboyantly dressed in a red suit with a purple scarf, Mavis was a stunning woman now in her early sixties, looking maybe forty, whose arched eyebrow could speak volumes and whose distinctive cackling laughter could, and did, stop people in their path.

We found a relatively quiet area in the airport, sat, and looked at each other in mutual delight. At my prompting she went first with the headlines of her life. They had renovated their upstate New York summer home, and she now lived there year-round. She was writing a political opinion column for the local newspaper, was active in local issues and global causes, and several times a year took the train into New York City for shopping and theater.

"And Mike?" I prompted.

"Oh, that ol' poop's still around. He's too mean to die."

"You're still married, then?"

"I figured you weren't when I looked in the phone book. I bet you were the one who decided to leave."

I was genuinely surprised. "Why do you assume that?"

"Girl, you were always so independent and strong-minded. And that man was pig-in-a-trough in love with you. He thought you peed champagne."

I would swear on a stack of women's magazines that in my marriage it was my husband who was the loved one, I the lover. Even after all these years of absorbing California consciousness along with the San Francisco fog, even having emerged from marriage into the single state in the 1970s with the support of thousands of media-hyped "sisters," it took some time for me to think of myself as strong and independent. How odd to see my young self and my marriage from such a perspective.

Conventions had changed, and our time together was limited, so I plunged right into pressing for details of her life and, most specifically, her feelings. She painted what I saw as a dismal picture. Neither she nor Mike had worked at a paying job for some years. She went to parties, to political functions, to her various volunteer causes, and Mike sat at home consuming at least one book and two six-packs of beer a day. "Girl," she laughed, "I bet I am the only individual in the history of humanity who went to a drive-in movie by herself. And then I had to get back early to fix his supper. I mean, he doesn't do one damn thing for himself. Sometimes I just hate that man."

"But why are you still married, then?"

She gave me a variety of "good" reasons—embers of old affection, the comfort of habit, companionship of a sort, no attractive alternatives, inertia, and ended with a casual . . . "and, of course, he doesn't ever bother me for his husband's rights in bed."

I was stunned into silence. She filled it with a barrage of questions about my life. I thought I presented a truthful and upbeat picture of a single working woman in the big city, but as I spoke I could see she was appalled. Having to meet bills and mortgage payments on my own? Sole responsibility for a child all those years? Coming home to an empty house after a disappointing date? Midnight heebie-jeebies faced alone in a solitary bed? "But you two got along so well. He never even drank. I don't understand why you left."

So I gave her my variety of "good" reasons—boredom, growing differences between us, differing interests and friends, the call of imagined possibilities elsewhere. "And," I finished, "I wanted more intimacy in my life, more sex."

She couldn't hide her shock. "Whatever for?"

There was, of course, no possible way to answer that. I tried for the general. "I'm happy, Mavis. I like my life. I wouldn't do anything differently if I could."

She shook her head, clucking over the uselessness of good advice given too late in the face of such recklessness. She, Mavis sighed, would never leave a perfectly good man and a perfectly good marriage for such paltry reasons and such pitiful so-called advantages.

In our less than two hours together, Mavis and I spoke more intimately than we ever had. Two modern women communicating in the modern manner. We parted with pleasure at renewing old ties, warm and dear friends . . . and two women further apart than New York and California and forty-some years.

I drove back from the airport, pulled the car into my garage, and unlocked the front door of my home. Silence greeted me—not empty, not lonely, a good silence. My home. Filled with things of my choosing collected from a life I enjoyed according to my own dictates. Every item in it, including my dozing cat, exactly as I left it when I received that surprising phone call less than three hours earlier.

"I do like my life," I said to myself, testing the truth of what I assured Mavis. In the many years since I left my marriage were there times I was lonely? Absolutely. And scared about money, too, and bringing up my daughter as a single parent, and occasionally entertaining the vision of every single woman's 3 a.m. bugaboo—ending up a broke and lonely bag lady. Yep. So did I regret choosing to be single? Not a whit; not even in the darkest of 3 a.m. scary scenarios.

I left a decent-enough marriage to a decent-enough man in order to seek more intimacy and more sex in my life. While not having it presented gift-wrapped by any sort of Prince Charming on white charger, I had managed to garner a goodly share of both over the years.

I said it. I meant it. I wouldn't do anything differently if I could. Sometimes it's very good to be reminded of that.

THE GLAMOROUS LIFE

Anne Buelteman

Pack up the luggage, la la la!
Unpack the luggage, la la la!
Pack up the luggage, la la la!
Hi ho the glamorous life!
—Stephen Sondheim

My favorite musical is Stephen Sondheim's *A Little Night Music*. His lyrics are often infused with the irony of experience, in this case, the experience of a life in the theater. The leading lady of the piece, the well-named actress Desiree, lists her itinerary as including Helsingborg, Rottvik, children with posies, mayors with speeches, and so on. She writes to her daughter, Fredrika, who is in the care of her grandmother while the so-desired Desiree traipses around the theaters of Scandinavia, leading what is ironically termed a "glamorous life." It's the turn of the last century, the musical is in waltz time, her admirers are dashing, and Desiree—after singing the beautiful "Send in the Clowns," about the bad timing in her personal life—ultimately has her cake and her old love, too.

Desiree's life is musical comedy, a sophisticated one, but a fantasy nonetheless, however self-mocking Mr. Sondheim's lyrics. My real life was lived for more than a decade with the national company of a Broadway musical, on tour in North America and occasionally Asia, fifty-two weeks a year for all that time. It was a life I chose for a number of reasons and stayed with longer than I ever imagined I would.

I am sometimes asked by friends and relatives about my long

159

years on the road. Apart from the obvious questions—how long, how many cities, how many suitcases—there's always the perplexity at my choice to, in essence, remove myself from any reasonable expectation of the "normal" life, the one with the house, the husband, the possible (although improbable) children, a "normal" career built by years of growth in one place. How could I stand being away so long? What about all the things I gave up by doing so?

Those questions and some of the others I have been asked, about artistic boredom, health issues, my sex life or not, money saved or spent, always make me pause and consider just exactly how rare or glamorous my life has been in recent years.

How long? Eleven years. How many cities? Three hundred twelve stops in 143 cities. Suitcases? Two, plus two carry-ons, until I started bringing my car along. As for the "normal" life I may or may not have left behind, when I hit the road at the age of forty-one, I believed it wasn't happening for me. California real estate was never going to be mine, and as for the men, the ones I wanted seldom wanted me, and when they did, it was generally a passing fancy. Finally, my chosen career—show biz—had been intermittently successful at best.

Of course, a life in the arts is usually not the most conventional of livings in any case. Consistent work is an often-unattainable dream, as is real estate. Personal relationships can be fleeting, if they happen at all, if the man turns out to be straight and unencumbered by wife or massive ego. This conclusion was reinforced once I began my odyssey. Furthermore, on the road, the progress of dozens of temporary relationships (a.k.a. "roadkill") from flirtation to fucking to fury was often played out in the public arena, whether hotel lobby, theater hallway, makeup station, or green room. Grab a seat and eat your popcorn, kids, Fred and Ginger are at it again! Yes, it could become tiresome, but admittedly I was nearly the grandma, considerably older than most of my coworkers and less entertained by (and presumably less prone to) public displays of personal drama.

Those bent on destroying or seriously compromising their marriages or other commitments were generally more discreet, although in such a goldfish bowl nothing remains secret for long. In the beginning, I was dismayed to hear of a young baritone whose fling with a musician segued into one with another young woman, an apparent amnesiac just back from her own honeymoon. Some little time later I was less surprised when one of the tenors became known as a "serial fiancé" after a succession of less-than-forever arrangements with newly hired ingénues. Eventually, the tale of a stagehand who seemed to be separated from his housebound wife, but, oddly, not when she came to visit, seemed more amusing than appalling, and I learned not to wince at the various (sometimes painfully) young women who arrived breathless and eager for a Showmance—whether or not there was a wife in the background.

There were occasional happy endings, too, although after the first several years, I began to hope that I wouldn't hear about it when a relationship broke up after the devoted pair left the road and tried life without room service for a few years. I did hear about it, too often. Interestingly, the gay partnerships fared marginally better than the straight ones. The breakups probably didn't exceed the national average, but sometimes it seemed that way. Of course, in the "normal" world you don't normally have an inescapable front-row seat for the disintegration of 50 percent of the relationships in your immediate circle. Oh, and those sweet and talented Mormon girls, married so young and breaking up when their husbands came out of the closet—that was another unfortunate boost to tour statistics.

So, relationships? Partnering? The cumulative effect of my experiences and observations before and after hitting the road was to support my conclusion that it wasn't meant for me and vice versa, probably because I had always expected so much from it: fidelity or, at the very least, the potential for something lasting. As for children, I had a niece and three nephews to satisfy any vestige of maternal instinct. The career—well, I was now having one, wasn't I, and the money was good enough to buy mutual funds, if not California real estate. My health was reasonably good, rheumatoid arthritis notwithstanding, my sex life . . . well, married flirts and the occasional sweetly inebriated stagehand were never quite enough, but that's life, isn't it?

As for the problem of artistic boredom, appearances to the contrary, there was quite a lot of variety in the job. The piece was based on a literary masterpiece and included a certain amount of nightly improvisation; it was, in fact, without the usual kick lines and choreographed moves of most musical blockbusters. The seventy-five members of the company, cast, crew, musicians, and management shuffled themselves in and out regularly, making it theoretically impossible to go on autopilot, as each show was a little new, a little different from the last. It is also possible to learn a great deal from watching the work of others, even if sometimes it is only what not to do. It can be, likewise, very entertaining.

That said, almost any job is better than no job in my business, especially if you have achieved an age where there are fewer jobs to be had all the time. The dearth of acting jobs for ordinary-looking women (not Goldie or Susan S., I mean) in their forties is a discussion I won't include here. If things got a little rough once in a while, my mantra became something like "Just one more year and you'll be a character actress!"

And from time to time, it did get a little rough. In the beginning, the downside of my glamorous life included several of Desiree's problems, the suitcases and the packing, and the "which town is this one?" It was probably at least a year before I had mastered my packing and located the optimum luggage and carry-ons. This is something that, believe it or not, became almost competitive—"Where did you get that rolling carry-on briefcase with the separate padded compartment for your computer and CD speakers?" And truly, there were times I would wake up in my room at the Ramada and lie there determined to remember on my own exactly which town in Ohio I was in, without resorting to the Filofax on the desk. But when, after several months I began to experience success in managing my belongings and the rest of my environment, constantly changing though they might be, I felt the high that only the dedicated organization freak (*not* control freak—I reject that) knows.

And yes, some weeks I got tired, and lonely, but often this fatigue followed encounters with (I'm sure perfectly lovely) people with "normal" lives—with airline personnel who overtly scoffed at my two large suitcases ("Two? What's wrong with you? Don't you know how to pack?") or hotel personnel who failed to understand the importance of a VCR hook-up ("A VCR? What's wrong with you? Can't you just watch the show when you get home next week?"). Or worse, persistent questioning by well-meaning friends outside the Biz—"Aren't you tired? Aren't you lonely?" After hearing it a few times I would consider (briefly) that maybe there was something wrong with me that I viewed the whole thing almost entirely in the light of a great adventure. In that way, the questions about loneliness were harder than loneliness itself. At fortysomething, loneliness was not an unknown, but I had friends enough, if not lovers, and was happy enough with myself to have come to the conclusion that, well, you either connect with people or you don't, they either understand you or they don't. And why should the Road be any different?

The thing is, the choices I made, the many little choices that led me, after my initial period of adjustment, to embrace a long-term nomadic existence, were not so very difficult for me after all. For a sometime drama queen, or at the very least as one who enjoys a good story, it would be satisfying to report that there was at some point a Dramatic Moment, a decision made with clarity about all the things I might be giving up. There was no such moment, no such drama.

There was, in essence, only me. The life suited me, and I believe vice versa. Baffling as my specific choices may be to some, the basic concept is simple and applies to each and every one of us.

It's no secret—one of the pleasures of getting older is the discovery that who you are, who you turned out to be, doesn't have to fit neatly into the conventional pictures of womanly (or even manly) accomplishment, old-fashioned or not. In my early forties I was coming to realize that I at last felt entitled to live my life the way it pleased me, and let friends and strangers term me "eccentric" if other definitions failed them. For all my early avowed belief in individualism, it took years to finally shed the last vestige of guilt or insecurity about not living a conventional, definable life. That freedom, that vision of myself, is the greatest gift, so far, of my middle age.

The greatest attraction for me was the bustle and motion of the life; the applause, the standing ovations, and the money were all great, but mostly, for better or worse, I loved the travel, the new places, and yes, the money to take the excursions, see the sights, eat at the restaurants, stay at the beach, and, of course, shop for the souvenirs. A life without a mortgage, however much one occasionally longs for a nest to return to—eventually—feels so very free. Call it wanderlust, an inquiring mind, or immaturity, self-absorption, emotional cowardice—it was ME.

As for my road longevity, there is a routine in this supposed lack of routine, and it becomes addictive. I mean, it either kills you early, or you have to have more of it. I had to have more of it— the rhythm of first nights and closings, six days on, one day off with a trip of up to seven hundred miles to the next town to accomplish, the occasional multiweek engagements, and the chance to really know a place, a neighborhood, the major cities of the continent, and the country in between. That part, the exploring part, ultimately kept me going long after I had imagined I would have gone home.

There was also a slightly addictive sense of pulling off a grand deception, and not just the onstage spectacle I helped to create. True, my backstage existence could sometimes be as surreal, odd, and stressful as a David Lynch movie, while what was onstage was still getting standing ovations. But beyond that, my extracurricular travels and activities allowed me to hold on to the conviction that, in the midst of a life that appeared to be equal parts overscheduled drudgery and frantic ersatz glamour, it was my choice, I who held the reins, and that I was, appearances perhaps to the contrary, both in control and freewheeling. (And I could quit any time I wanted to, but I didn't want to!)

And oh, those cities; oh, those days and nights off. Great meals, boat rides, hikes, and drives. In Annapolis, I took a refresher course in small-boat sailing. I loved getting out on the water whenever possible and took excursions in Marblehead and Sanibel Island, and once in Singapore we went sailing at midnight under the classic full moon. Seventy-eight degrees, light wind with mingled scents of brine and onshore tropical flowers, French bread, wine, and Brie, and Watsonville strawberries from the gourmet market on Orchard Road. There was horseback riding in Park City and in Tucson among the majestic and phallic saguaros, and snorkeling on an almost completely deserted island off the Malay Peninsula after a hike up a palm-studded ridge looking down on impossibly clear blue water.

I sipped midnight poolside cocktails at the Delano in Miami Beach, which involved group lounging on a twelve-foot-wide canvas tuffet and spilling over onto the lawn around it.

There was also Harry's bar on the boat quay in Singapore, with the world's oiliest peanuts and seven-dollar beers you didn't mind paying for, and smoky jazz featuring a sexy strong-nosed

Frenchman on the sax, and afterward a plate of penne pomodoro next door at Pasta Fresca until 4 a.m. And in Austin, as in Fort Worth or Memphis, I sat with eyes closed, listening to the local blues brothers and cheering the occasional sit-in performance by one of our own wonderful musicians.

In company with a few close women friends, usually older like me, I regularly relished the genteel self-indulgence of afternoon tea, individual pots of Darjeeling and Lapsang souchong, tiny sandwiches, scones and clotted cream, fruit-and-custard tarts, and, in those particularly stressful weeks, one glass of champagne. Lots of laughs, sympathetic talk, pretty dresses, and at the Peabody in Memphis, one of our favorites, a parade of ducks from their courtyard fountain, where they splashed all day, to the private elevator to their penthouse on the roof.

I enjoyed my excursions with friends, but took many of my intercity drives and side trips alone, relishing the feeling of solo exploration. I remember a dip at the Mount Princeton Hot Springs in Colorado, lying in a natural-rock pool of geothermal hot water bubbling up at the very edge of a creek full of melted snow, the two extreme temperatures washing over me in small slow waves and disconnecting my mind from my usual trains of thought. Once I took an air-taxi hop from Vancouver to Salt Spring Island, over its mountainous ridge and miles of pristine-appearing evergreen forests, and more than once I drove Route 1 all the way down the Florida keys, opalescent water lapping either side of my road and a nearly Caribbean island at the end of it. In Sedona and Moab, I hiked up red rock ridges and through desert arch formations, climbing to the top of a mesa to sit on the edge and stare at the photograph-defying surroundings and to eat my deli sandwich in the oppressive, somehow enjoyable heat. And once I walked part of the Great Wall of China discussing some history and a little politics with my twenty-five-year-old Beijing university student guide.

Those adventures and my love of fine dining may have cut into the bottom line of my mutual fund account, but they made the trip worth taking. In the dark-paneled dining room of the Old Ebbitt Grill, across from the White House, I sensed the pulse of power (testosterone? megalomania?) all around me. A late plate of house-made cannelloni or a snifter of something from the extensive after-dinner list felt oh-so-civilized after an evening spent running around in the dark, repeatedly taking my clothes off and putting them on again. (Hi ho. . .) Another week in San Antonio, I relished the spicy Indian food at Simi's and was given a tour of the tandoor oven and a demonstration of how the naan bread is made. There were tasty escargots at Gibby's in old Montreal, and tasty ballplayers at the Pink Pony in Scottsdale. And one evening at M on the Bund in Shanghai, I savored an amazing house-smoked salmon with a black caviar sabayon while from the sleek dining room I watched the floodlit modern skyline across the Huangpu River. Sounds from the balcony made me imagine the Victorian promenade below us alive with people strolling along the row of colonial-era banks, trading houses, consulates, and hotels, walking alongside the ghosts of adventurers, notorious beauties, millionaires, and entrepreneurs from the 30s.

A couple of engagements in New Orleans served to further my quest for great culinary breaks. There were, not surprisingly, delicious meals to be had at the famous restaurants, but I especially remember agreeably settling a backstage argument with a sound technician about grits. In an old working-class neighborhood literally across the street from a levee higher than the rooftop, I found a breakfast café named Elizabeth's—an older building, a plain room with dinettes and a ceiling fan, and an eggs-and-bacon meal including real old-fashioned, creamy, slow-cooked grits better even than my grandma made. Real artery-choking stuff and no fancy French name to pronounce.

Occasional honors also came my/our way, local and international—I actually gave a short interview in French for a Regina, Saskatchewan, radio station. I sang (with a group) the national anthem at Camden Yards in Baltimore, Mile High Stadium in Denver, and SBC Park in San Francisco. I felt I was a little part of history when, on our opening night in Shanghai, there was an audible gasp over our first-act finale and at the end Communist Party leaders, floodlit by TV news cameras, gave us a standing ovation. In Washington, D.C., we met the Clintons and spent one Fourth of July on the White House lawn; another Fourth, I walked the Freedom Trail in Boston, to the accompaniment of a youth brass band playing "What Is Hip?" as it marched past the Granary Burying Ground where Hancock and Paine are buried, and later walked over to the Esplanade to take in the chaos of the annual Boston Pops concert, timing it so that by the time I inched my way up to within two hundred yards or so of the band shell, they were doing the *1812 Overture*, complete with cannons and fireworks.

Who could resist a life that includes such beauties and absurdities—certainly not I! Of course, driving the old stagecoach road from Colorado Springs to Cripple Creek, about thirty-five miles of dirt road and wonderful views at eight to ten thousand feet, I ended up with a flat tire, and did so again outside Birmingham, Alabama. Once, about forty miles outside Boise, I had a blowout that ignited a small and mercifully short-lived brush fire, and rode twelve miles in a pickup truck with a friendly stranger to get a tow. (This was before cell phones.) Other what-the-hell-are-we-doing-here moments included the Scranton Anthracite Heritage Museum, the "What Is Plutonium?" display at the airport in Amarillo, and the edifying discovery that Muncie, Indiana, is most famous for Ball State University, named after the man who invented Ball jars for canning fruit. There were three tornados in our vicinity one month in Florida, an earthquake in

Pasadena, the monsoon season in Singapore, and a plague of cicadas in Nashville. Not always the smoothest of odysseys, but always my own.

I am not sure that any of us can fully comprehend another's choices without standing in her shoes, and although my tales of the road are generally well received by my friends and other listeners, I am often left with the feeling that I am regarded as some kind of congenial and entertaining freak or exotic creature. I believe that at heart I am not so very different, even though my personal solutions for life's challenges may be. And I know this kind of incomprehension is a two-way street. I like to think that I do understand the many attractions of a more conventional life lived in one place, the comfort of a partner who shares your joys, and presumably your responsibilities, the opportunity to be part of a child's life, the home that grows and changes through the accumulation of things that matter to you, a garden to sit in, a community to be part of, walk-in closets, and Christmas cards you actually send out on time. I have wanted all those things from time to time, and in some measure, I still do.

But this other life, this "glamorous life" with its literal baggage and constant motion, has allowed me to be who I am best, to fit into a larger world, where a smaller, perhaps dearer world has eluded me. The opportunity was a blessing, and being over forty allowed me to embrace it with avidity and, most of the time, a sense of humor. And to realize, perhaps not for the first time, that in choosing as I did, I chose myself.

CUTTING LOOSE

Jane Juska

J udith sits across the table from me at the café. We have not met before; I am here at the behest of Judith's friend, whom I know slightly and who assures me that reading my book, about what happened when I advertised for sex at the age of 67 in the *New York Review of Books*, has changed Judith's life. "Please," the friend urges, "talk to her."

Judith looks as if her life needs to be changed. She is pinched all over, like a raisin, like a little worm that shrinks at the sign of danger. She is fifty-seven going on sixty-nine. She looks over her bifocals at me and tells me her life: Judith is long divorced; her two sons are grown and far away; she teaches fifth grade in an inner-city school; she is lonely and, as we talk, desperate for the company of a man who might lessen the misery of her life.

"I have not been with a man in many years," she says shame-facedly. "When I read your book, I thought, That's me." Then she looks at me full on and asks, "Do you have any suggestions?"

Judith sits slumped in her chair, her shoulders rounded, both hands warming themselves on her coffee mug, her blue eyes alight with hope. That's it: my book seems to have given many people hope and, with so little of it in the world these days, I am happy that hope flies out of my book and into the lives of people who want it. Judith, however, is not about to be satisfied with hope; she wants details; she wants explanations, a plan for the future.

I lean across the table and say, "Lighten up."

I've done it now, no going back: "It seems to me we jump to the end too quickly; we tell ourselves we want a mate for life, a man who will be a companion and lover and who will stay with us, never abandon us, until death do us part."

Judith nods, downcast.

"That's asking a lot," I say. "If I were a man sitting here right now, I'd get up and run." She's still nodding; I plunge ahead: "We forget to have fun. We're so intent on ending up not alone we miss out on what can come before the end, and sometimes, in our desperation, we drown the possibilities of life."

I am aghast at myself; I have delivered a sermon. Judith rises and says, "Maybe," and "Thanks." I mutter something about going online, wish her good luck, and off we go. To what or to whom is up to chance and as much common sense as we can muster.

I do think that we women shoot ourselves in the foot when we go in search of a man, when we find one who just might do. Most of us are so dedicated to the idea of commitment—the longer the term the better—that the idea of just having a good time never gets a chance to bloom. As a woman in her seventies, I am not interested in long-term commitment, and I'll bet I can safely say this is true of others of my age. We have learned to take care of ourselves and, along the way, have become fully aware that each day is a gift, that we are grateful for it and happy for a man to share it.

However, no woman I know who is my age wants to get married, though here I suppose I had better speak for myself: the possibility of having to ingratiate myself with a family of strangers—my new husband's—does not please me. Somewhere from the throng of adult children and grandchildren a bad seed will arise whose chief purpose in life is to make my life miserable. I've seen it happen. The possibility of taking over the management of a household—perhaps cooking regularly, laundering a pile of boxer shorts and T-shirts—does not excite me, nor does scrubbing the bathroom tile around the base of the toilet.

Most of us single women have made fairly good lives for ourselves. We live modestly but comfortably, we travel a bit, we dine in fairly good restaurants, and some of us even have cleaning women. Now, I could get excited about marrying a wealthy man, I suppose, someone whose cook and housekeeper and laundress and driver (not all the same person, mind you) would cosset me in ways I so richly deserve. But throughout my post-divorce single life of some forty years, people have asked, "Don't you want to get married again?" My answer remains the same: "I don't know anyone I want to marry."

This does not mean "I do not want to make love." It took me years to understand that making love and getting married were not synonymous or consecutive or even necessarily related.

Recently, a friend who is writing a book about the erotic lives of seniors told me that in his research he has met many women in their late sixties and seventies and older whose sex lives are rich and full; these, he told me, appear to be happy women. On the other hand, his interviews of unpartnered women in their forties and fifties reveal them to be, by and large, miserable. This is understandable, for as a young fifty-year-old divorced neighbor said to me, "I have a long life ahead of me, and I want to live it with someone who is committed to the same thing." Well, there it is again—commitment—and, of course, wouldn't it be nice.

But it's sort of putting the cart before the horse. When we were in our twenties and thirties, we wanted a husband to father our children; we wanted someone to help rear them, to help support them, to offer strength and reassurance. This makes a lot of evolutionary sense. But once our childbearing years are behind us, what do we want a man to commit himself to? Us? A bit presumptuous, don't you think? Not impossible, of course, not after he comes to know and to love us. But right off the bat? And if commitment is uppermost in our minds, "right off the bat" is going to show itself on our faces and in the way we carry ourselves and in what we say and do, and we are doomed. I side with the man in this case. Neediness is not attractive.

Back to Judith: I am in the post office, and there stands Judith. She is trim in Levi's and sweater, her blue eyes bright and happy, her smile wide and genuine. "I did what you suggested," she says. "I went online. And I found someone."

Well, good for her.

"For a while things were great, but then he wanted me to change my life." Words rush from her. "He wanted me to quit my job, to travel with him, to move into his house." She takes a breath and races through to the end. "And suddenly, I thought, gee, I like my job, I like my friends, I like my apartment. And so I said no. I said, 'Thanks, but no thanks.'"

We leave the post office together, and Judith says, "Life is good, you know?" And off she goes into the sunshine, a free woman.

THe OPeN NeST

Sam Horn

While I was walking my dog Murph around our lake, a neighbor stopped and asked, "How are your sons doing? I haven't seen them around lately."

"They're both off to college," I explained. "Tom's a junior at Virginia Tech, and Andrew left a few weeks ago for Providence."

"Ooooh," she said sympathetically, patting me on the shoulder. "You must be suffering from empty nest syndrome. I know how lonely it is to rattle around an empty house."

I looked at her in surprise. The thought had never occurred to me.

During the next few weeks, a number of other acquaintances solicitously asked how I was doing, assuming I was incapacitated by the "loss" of my two sons.

Frankly, I don't see my teenagers leaving home as a sad occurrence. They're doing exactly what I raised them to do. My goal was for them to become self-sufficient human beings who went off into the world to make their own way. This is a time for celebration, not depression.

Don't get me wrong. I miss my sons. I miss their humor, quick minds, and everyday presence. However, I have my own life. As long as I know they're healthy, surrounded by friends, learning new things, and taking care of themselves, I'm happy for them.

It's my turn now. I've willingly put Tom and Andrew first for the past two decades. My primary responsibilities were getting them to and from school and sports, setting up birthday parties and sleepovers, welcoming their pals into our home, mediating squabbles, reading bedtime stories, giving nightly back rubs, sharing discoveries, answering questions, reveling in their inquisitive minds, holding them accountable for chores, homework, and so on. I have enjoyed almost (let's be honest here) every minute of it.

We were fortunate in that we lived on Maui for the first twelve years of their lives. Getting to the beach three or four times a week became a pleasant necessity. There, Tom and Andrew could run, wrestle, yell at the top of their lungs, build things and knock them down—in other words, be boys—without my having to rein them in.

They would dash into the kid-friendly surf with their boogie boards, ride the waves all the way in until they scraped their bellies on the beach, and then jump up and do it all over again. They were the epitome of healthy youthful exuberance. Their full-out joy filled me with gratitude at how fortunate I felt to be their mom.

People walking by would often pause to watch, and I would ask if they had any advice for a mother with two young children. One grandmother told me, "When it comes to kids, remember, it's long days, short years. One day, they're driving you crazy with their constant demands for attention and the next they're out on their own. Be grateful for each day instead of wishing them away."

I took her advice to heart. I'm convinced it is one of the reasons I don't have regrets now that the boys are in college. I don't see them as being "gone." I still talk with them on the phone. I still hear news of girlfriends, grades, and cars. My older son IM's me to share his excitement about being given the key to the university's observatory (he who twelve years ago used to look up at the stars on our nightly walk-and-rolls in Maui and say, "When I grow up, I want to do something with 'up there.'") I get an excited phone call about the hard-earned B (in calculus, no less) from my younger son, who hates math. Just because I don't see them on a daily basis doesn't mean they're not in my life.

I asked a friend how she felt about her only child moving across the country to attend a major college on an athletic scholarship. She said, "A client asked if I was suffering from empty nest syndrome. To tell you the truth, I was kind of insulted. *Empty* means no one lives in our house. Joe and I are still here. Don't we count?"

Good point. I suggest that we, as individuals and a society, change the language around this issue. The words we use to *describe* an experience *define* that experience. *Empty* means "blank, vacant, unoccupied, abandoned, deserted, unfulfilled, uninhabited." Yikes. All negative connotations. If we continue to use that odious cliché "empty nest syndrome," we will indeed dread this passage and see ourselves as being bereft.

I propose we replace "empty nest syndrome" with "*open* nest syndrome." *Open* is defined as "release, free, liberate, limitless, uninhibited." What a difference a word can make.

You may be thinking, "This is sounding a little Pollyanna-ish for me. Changing a word isn't going to change the way I feel about my kids being gone."

Au contraire. Our greatest philosophers, from Gandhi to Socrates, have all agreed that changing our words changes our perceptions, which changes our feelings. Adopting the phrase "open nest syndrome" can help us see that our home isn't unoccupied; it's home base. Instead of being where we all reside, it's where we all reconvene.

The benefits of an "open nest" approach were brought home (so to speak) three weeks after my younger son left for college. For the past twenty years, I had been the traveling equivalent of a maternal rubber band. I would fly to a speaking engagement and then return home as soon as my presentation was over. After my son left, I was booking a business trip to Cancún and asking the airline rep for the next flight back when a little voice piped up, "Why rush home?"

That's why, a month later, you could have found me stretched out by the pool, basking in the warm sunshine of Cancún instead of battling the zero-degree temperatures and icy sidewalks of Washington, D.C. What a concept. Now, instead of automatically jumping on the next flight home, I ask myself, "What else would I like to do and who else would I like to see while I'm here?"

A friend told me, "I agree with this intellectually, but I'm having a hard time pulling this off emotionally. It's been so long since I've put myself first, I've forgotten how."

I told her I understood and gifted her with a list of my favorite inspirational "open nest" quotes. I confessed that every once in a while, usually on a Friday or Saturday night if I haven't planned anything, I feel a little adrift. That's when I walk over and look at the quotes that I keep on my refrigerator.

"To wait for someone else to make my life richer, fuller, or more satisfying puts me in a constant state of suspension."—Kathleen Tierney Andrus

"No one with a good hobby is ever lonely for long."—Beran Wolfe, M.D.

"Your future depends on many things, but mostly it depends on you."—F. Tyger

"The amount of satisfaction you get from life depends largely on your own ingenuity, self-sufficiency, and resourcefulness. People who wait around for life to supply their satisfaction usually find boredom instead."—William Menninger

"You have to own your days and live them, each one of

them, every one of them, or else the years go right by and none of them belong to you."—H. Gardner

These quotes are tangible reminders that my life isn't empty, it's wide open. That's not a platitude; it's a reality if I remind myself that friends are a phone call away. Adventure is waiting outside my front door. These quotes get me up and outside, where I once again realize a big world is waiting for me to take advantage of it. All I have to do is remember Anaïs Nin's advice, "Life expands or contracts in proportion to one's courage" and initiate on my own behalf.

5.

OTHER KINDS OF LOVE

Our World . . . Our Dependents . . . Ourselves

There is a fountain of youth: it is your mind, your talents,
the creativity you bring to your life and the lives of
people you love. When you learn to tap this source,
you will truly have defeated age.

—Sophia Loren

I don't need a man to rectify my existence. The most profound relationship we'll ever have is the one with ourselves.

—Shirley MacLaine

A secret joy

Susan Griffin

The first time was difficult. I did not plan to end up alone in a hotel in Europe. Twenty years ago, the idea of traveling unaccompanied had no appeal at all for me. This was one of those periods in my life (such as I am experiencing now) when I had no husband, no wife, not even a love affair. Still, I wanted to take advantage of the round-trip ticket I had been given to Europe. After lecturing in Amsterdam, I planned to fly to Nice. There is a hotel that I love near there in the low mountain range, just behind the city, called the Maritime Alps.

Though the Colombe d'Or is a cherished landmark of art history with a famous restaurant, it was by accident that I discovered the hotel more than twenty years ago. My partner and I were on a train traveling from Italy to France when we decided to stay in the South of France for a few days before returning to Paris. We had no more particular destination in mind. But leafing through a popular book that reprinted the recommendations of other travelers, we came upon an intriguing description of this hotel. Noisy bar, it said, but good food and atmosphere. I had no idea that I was heading toward what I consider a minor paradise. An old Provençal house, rooms filled with antiques. A long pool lined with green tile, lemon trees and sculpture around it, a mobile by

Calder hanging over it. A terrace flanked by a medieval city wall on one side, a mural by Léger at the back, a view of green hills and stucco *bastides* in front of us. The single night it rained we dined inside, in a room with wonderful old wood wainscoting, paintings by Braque and Picasso on the walls. This was the place that local artists, in the days before they were famous, came to drink. They paid their mounting bar bills with art work. I wanted to return.

After my lecture in Amsterdam, I traveled to Saint-Paul-de-Vence, where I joined friends at the hotel for a weekend, following which I had decided to stay on for five more days with a close Parisian friend who was planning to come at the beginning of the week. But just before the first round of friends left, I got a call from her. Her knee was giving her trouble. She was advised not to travel. This brought about my first experience dining alone in a fine restaurant.

Though they were slow, the days were not as difficult. I had no car, but there were galleries within walking distance in the area I wanted to revisit. I went swimming, lingered by the pool, read, walked in the village, and found some used silver at a shop, aging pieces that must have been relinquished by the hotel. The challenge came at night. When I look back, it seems like a scene from an old movie, one where the heroine has been abandoned, with tragically sad results. I dressed carefully for the nine o'clock meal, only to sit by myself at the table reserved for me, on a terrace filled with conversation, flirtation, and laughter. Feeling conspicuously uncoupled, I even envied the little quarrels I witnessed.

I have come to see how complex loneliness is. To eat at home alone has never bothered me. Sitting in a restaurant comfortably by myself, however, was an entirely different matter. In the first place there is the imagined tyranny of others, what they think, what you think they think, their pity, the conclusions they might draw. In the shadow of the custom of sharing meals in restaurants with others, the wallflower syndrome is activated—not only the sting of not being chosen but also the shame of it. And this is just one of many possible layers in endless permutations of consciousness. As I sat on that gloriously beautiful terrace in the Maritime Alps, ghosts of loneliness from the past began to haunt me. That at the age of six I had lost everyone in my immediate family through divorce entered me not so much as fact or even awareness, but rather as a bodily feeling, an unnamed vacuum into which I was descending again despite all my best efforts. Incipient tears mixed with the desire to repress them only intensified my misery.

I was given more than one reprieve during that visit. For two consecutive evenings I joined the table of another single woman whom I had met by the pool. I am still not fluent in French, was then even less so, and she had no English. But we were glad to try bits of conversation. Then an old friend who was in the area came to take me to the Côte d'Azur for a meal. And, finally, two American couples whom I enjoyed immensely invited me to join them at dinner for the rest of my stay.

From this experience one might suppose I would not choose to travel alone again. But I did. And from each of these journeys the seed of a different experience began to grow in me. There was the time, for instance, that I had arranged to arrive in Aix three days before meeting a friend there. For various reasons, though we remain friends, we did not do well as traveling companions. She had recently decided she needed to be more assertive and, like any other novice, was not very graceful with her new posture. But I was not innocent either. In the days I spent alone there, a profound shift was taking place in me, too, one I had not even named. I walked slowly in the gardens of the hotel. Strolled through Aix. Savored my meals in the garden alone with great pleasure. I had been to several other European cities doing emotionally painful and exhausting research, and now I soaked up the beauty, the silence, and the solitude, yes, solitude, as a precariously thirsty woman coming out of a desert might welcome water.

The expectations of culture have a powerful influence on even the most private feelings. I have always loved to walk alone. At times I take walks with friends, but even though I work alone much of the day, I thrive on the particular kind of solitude I experience while walking, whether hiking a trail on Mount Tamalpais across the bay from where I live, or covering twenty-five blocks in New York City. Yet it took me years to discover the same joy eating in a restaurant alone.

On subsequent trips in France (where I usually take my vacations) I had two encounters that seem to me now to be part of this story. On the first occasion I had driven to a restaurant in a very small village I love in the Luberon. It was summertime, and the evening was long and lovely. I chose to eat at an old and well-known restaurant in town, which had an outdoor terrace. At 9 p.m., it was still very light and warm. Two women close to my age were seated at a table near me. Because they looked toward me as they spoke, I could tell they were discussing me. They smiled and I smiled back, but we exchanged no words. By then I had learned to enjoy taking a meal by myself, and I returned to that pleasure. After my half carafe of wine had come, and between my first and second courses, they got up to leave. One of them approached my table and leaned over to speak to me. "I just wanted to tell you," she said in French, "how much we admire you for taking yourself out to dinner. Bravo, you have inspired us," she said triumphantly, as she left.

On another trip to the South of France, in the course of doing research on a different book, I rented a car and drove from Aix to to Saintt-Maximum so that I could participate in an annual ceremony at the cathedral there. The church claims to possess the skull of Mary Magdalene. In an annual procession, this holy relic is moved from the basilica to a convent just over a kilometer away. While studying the black skull in its golden casing, which is temporarily opened for a few hours before the procession, I found myself surrounded by a group of American pilgrims. Two of them were having difficulty reading the French placards that described the history of the skull. After I told them where they could find Magdalene's crypt and translated the commentary for them, they began to ask me questions. Who was I with? Why was I there? Where was I staying? I told them that I was staying in a hotel in Aix, that I had come for the ceremony, that I was not Catholic but was interested in the Magdalene, and that I had come to Provence and driven across the Var to Saint-Maximum alone.

I might as well have told them that I had come by myself across the Sahara on a camel. Astonished and intrigued, they invited me to have dinner with them. Their tour guide, they said, was taking them to a pasta place. But always a lover of food, I did not find this idea appealing. "We're in France," I said. "And I have a good nose for restaurants. Why don't you come with me?" After conferring with each other and their guide, they agreed. They had wanted to try French food, they said, but their guide always took them for pasta or pizza.

A secret joy of traveling alone is that occasionally you find yourself spending time with people you would not otherwise get to know. They were older than I was, religious, married, and fairly conventional, best friends from a small town in Ohio. But we shared a memorable evening. I found a very good restaurant, talked the proprietors into serving us early (since we would be very grateful, and after all, we wanted to go to an important service at the town's great basilica), and, since they did not know French food, helped them to order. Because melon served with Beaume de Venise was on the menu, I suggested we all might order it as the first course. They were not sure melon would be special enough, but I assured them that since it was from Cavaillon, which produces the best melons in France, and because this was the proper season, it would be spectacular. As is usual in France, especially in the countryside, the restaurant took a while to take our orders and then to fulfill them. One of my new friends was quite worried we would be late for the service. But her worry vanished shortly after the first course arrived. When the first taste of melon reached her palate, her eyes got as big as saucers. After two more bites, and several more sips of wine, she said with a tone of unmistakable insouciance, "Oh, what difference does it make if we're a little late? We really don't have to go at all!"

By the time we had finished our duck with lavender honey and we had decided we could not pass up dessert, we had become old friends. I listened to them both describe their devotion to Mary Magdalene and then described my own spirituality, in Presbyterian Sunday school, and later, perhaps because as a teenager I was adopted by secular Jewish parents, an interest in Jewish mysticism, seasoned with Buddhist practice and, of course, my own fascination with the Magdalene. We had each had more wine than we were used to consuming. I told them I thought that eating a meal was as much a religious experience as any and that it was truly in the spirit of Mary Magdalene. They heartily agreed.

Indeed, the unexpected delight of the meal we shared and our newfound friendship colored the walk we took, in a procession from the basilica to the convent, with a flush of slightly outré pleasure. And for my part, I found myself entering into the spirit of their devotion, experiencing the candlelight of the worshippers, the choir at the convent, the beatitudes the monk read, the very beautiful verdigris-covered statue of the Virgin Mary, opposite which the Magdalene's skull was placed, all through their eyes as well as my own. It was truly a blessed event, one I would never have known had I not traveled alone.

Solitary travel is not always perfect. It has its downfalls, drawbacks. Moments of true loneliness, when the desire to talk to another human being becomes very strong; moments of fear, when you wish you had someone to help you cope with road maps and hairpin turns and barking dogs or rude waiters. But so does traveling with another person, lover or friend, group or circle, have its drawbacks. Opposing desires, conflicting choices and tastes, one who talks too much or whom you find too industrious, moving rapidly from site to site, seemingly incapable of resting at the cafés you long to inhabit, or another who seems to have no curiosity at all and wants to stay barricaded in a hotel room all day. Both ways of traveling, alone or in tandem, have their difficulties; they are simply different difficulties.

A man reading this account may find it silly. For generations men have been born with the right to travel alone, to be intrepid adventurers, to risk unknown territories for the sake of discovery. But most women will understand the struggle I encountered within myself to win this right and all the freedom from the unreasonable fear and false constriction it implies.

The last experience I want to include in my traveler's tale occurred the summer before last, when I decided I wanted to see the Basque region. I stayed for a few days at the coast in Saint-Jean-de-Luz and then went inland to see smaller villages and walk in the Pyrenees. Again I met people when I was there whom I enjoyed immensely. But given my own internal voyage, one of the more remarkable experiences I had was the displeasure I felt one night when my solitude was interrupted. I had chosen my hotel carefully, an affordable place, built in the seventeenth century, with a good view and a good kitchen. From years of traveling in the countryside of France, I have grown to love the comfort of an auberge where you can eat your evening meal and then, without having to drive anywhere, simply retire to your room. This hotel had wonderful food served on a lovely terrace under wide old plane trees, next to a running stream (where some of the fish we ate were caught) that ran under an old stone bridge. After two nights as a guest I had graduated to a table right by the edge of the water. Then, on my last night, the waiter told me that a couple at another table had asked if perhaps I didn't want some company. I should have listened to him when he said to me, "You can say no, if you like." What I did say was that I preferred to be alone until dessert and that when it was served I would come to their table.

My message was not communicated accurately or else it was ignored, and I suspect the latter was true. Because the couple, whom I had greeted but not gotten to know before at all, were not obnoxious so much as impervious to everything. They could not really appreciate or even fathom the culture that surrounded them, added to which they were—there is no polite way to say it— very boring. I almost always find something interesting if not compelling in the stories others tell about their lives, but, at least in our exchange, they turned the same unseeing eyes through which they encountered the world toward themselves, too. Unfortunately, they came to my table during the main course, spoiling the last hour I had to spend by myself with the river and the trees and the sweet murmur of voices around me.

But this is really the point. I had finally learned to treasure that hour, that fading light, the reflection in the water, and the way I could gaze without distraction, letting the beauty pull me into memory or insight and that particular rapture that belongs only to solitude.

Heavy Petting

Rachel Toor

For the first time in my adult life I am not only single, I am alone. For the first time in two decades, when I come home at the end of the day, there's no one for me to tell it to, no one to greet me; there's no one to recognize and claim me. Frankly, it sucks. But I know it will be temporary. I am certain of this.

I have been married and divorced, gone on a gazillion dates, lived with men, and done the messy shuttle between houses where toothbrushes and stray pairs of underwear lay claim to territorial rights. I've loved a bucketload of guys and been loved right back.

The men have come and gone (sometimes for good reasons, sometimes not); what I've always relied on, though, counted on and been sustained by, has been the constant love of a good pet.

There are lots of jokes about women who end up living with cats after giving up on finding a man. When a thirtysomething woman shows off wallet photos of her dog, many think: Oh, poor thing, she really wants a baby. For some reason, people like to believe that those of us who love animals are kidding ourselves, that we either can't have—or don't want—a "real" relationship. That is, a relationship with a member of our own species.

The truth is, my first love was a mutt named Barkus. From her I learned about tolerance and patience, acceptance and loyalty.

To her I gave unqualified, unfettered love. For many years I've sought a man whom I could love as freely, as generously and unequivocally, as I loved Barkus.

The uninitiated might joke that it's easy to love a pet, because "it" can't talk back (they will say *it* rather than he or she). They'll say that loving an animal is about projection, control, about never having to compromise. Those who haven't lived with pets tend to flatten the rough terrain of individuality into broad and unfair generalizations. ("Dogs are followers," they'll say. "Cats are unpredictable," they'll claim.)

Those of us who love animals know the vast and various ways in which you come to resemble your pets. I can think of nothing more heartwarming than the sight of an old man hobbling down a street dogged by an equally ancient nonhuman companion, both weathered, both grown lighter in hair and heavier in bulk with age, shuffling the same shuffle they do every day, performing a ritual that is as profound for them as churchgoing. Slim young women walk whippet-thin dogs dressed in matching Burberry coats up and down the streets of New York. Framed photos of pets—cats, dogs, horses, birds—peer out from desktops everywhere. Either you can see yourself across species, or you can't. Either you get it, or you don't.

In college I bummed dogs like cigarettes. Without a pack of my own, I had to beg and borrow to get my fix of canine company. After I'd been addicted to animals my whole life, leaving for school meant going cold turkey on the pet front. I learned to comfort myself with the next best thing: men.

But by my last year in college, when late-night hookups proved emotionally unsatisfying and I was living for the first time in a single room, with no roommates to come home to, I wanted company. In the shadows of the ivy-covered ivory tower, I wanted to feel less small. I needed . . . what? I needed a pet. But what? Who could live with me in a tiny dorm room? Who wouldn't get me kicked out of school just prior to earning a degree? Who could be as quiet . . . as quiet as . . . as a mouse! A mouse.

I named her Prudence. It shouldn't count as a virtue, since as virtues go, prudence is a mousely one, just as gluttony is a silly sin. Plus, I liked that her name was longer than she.

Prudence's fur was as soft as baby powder, talcy white. Her eyes were red beads, not unlike precious round rubies. Her ears were thin to the point of translucence, mapped lightly with delicate spidery veins. She had exquisitely tiny nails and long, elegant whiskers. She was a clean and tidy mouse, never peeing or pooping except in her cage. Whenever I was in my dorm room, I would prop open her door and let her explore or stay in, as she pleased.

I would sit at my desk, and she would run around it, checking out messy sheaves of paper, climbing alpine piles of books. As I wrote my papers on a cheap plastic portable Smith-Corona, Prudence liked to crawl on the keys, chasing after my fingers as they flew quickly in fits and starts. She'd climb onto the tops of my hands, and I would stop, turning them over to palm her. I loved it when she'd interrupt my work like this. I loved that she would seek me out.

I stroked her cheek, and she would lean, exposing so much of it to my finger that eventually she'd keel over onto her side, one front paw near her face, a back foot stretched out like a ballet dancer's. Prudence became my life that last semester. My biggest love affair in college was with someone who weighed less than a Snickers bar.

After graduation I moved to New York and met a man. Charlie offered good looks, unstinting enthusiasm, a big heart, a hard body, and an apartment that was great in the three most important features of real estate: location, location, location. Prudence and I moved in with him.

Charlie was loving. He was considerate. He was generous, funny, and eager to please. He had money, and he shared it freely.

But even as he found ways to accommodate me, I felt trapped. Charlie's need was so great—he wanted to be liked, he wanted to be funny, he wanted to be wanted. He worked so hard to please me that I became exasperated and worn down. And anything but pleased. He was a small man, and he brought out all of my own smallness.

Prudence died. I dumped Charlie.

After that I got Hester, a rat, and Vince, a new boyfriend, who was smart and edgy and demanding. Hester and I battled (I thought she was a bitch) until I learned to see—and accept—her for who and what she was. Vince and I got along (I thought he was brilliant) until I saw that his intense jealousy and need to know where I was every moment of every day, to change the way I dressed and talked and interacted with friends was, well, not so good.

Hester died. I dumped Vince.

I met Patrick in a bar in Brooklyn. He was big and solid and soft-spoken, a handsome big-headed man like you find in adventure films. We dated, fell in love, and he asked me to move in. If I lived with him, he said, we could get a dog.

Hannah matured into sixty solid pounds, with a barrel chest and thin, elegant legs; a thinking dog, she was perfectly capable of kicking up her heels and having fun but, from her earliest days, was fundamentally serious.

She waited patiently each morning until there were signs of life coming from our bed. Then she'd pop up and settle herself between Patrick and me, lying lengthwise, head on the pillow. She'd greet the dawn and us with a howl all her own. She would sing, and we'd join her, each of us yodeling at 7 a.m. Patrick would grind her ears, and she'd coo. I'd wrap my arms around my sweet, smart dog and my big, gentle boyfriend and think that this was the life I'd always wanted.

We loved each other. We married. We grew apart. Patrick and

I wanted different things; our dreams spun out in different directions. He was a great guy, but he wasn't, finally, the guy for me. Sometimes, what you think you want isn't what you want at all.

But over the next seventeen years I never fell out of love with Hannah. When you love animals, you never have to deal with conflicting goals, clashing agendas. Constancy and forgiveness are among the many gifts of loving a pet. Humans change. It makes staying in love both more fulfilling and harder.

I moved to North Carolina and met Jonathan. There are plenty of smart people in the world. But to love the way someone's mind zigs and zags, to know that every story is worth listening to, that after each movie you see together he will point out something you've missed, to have someone who can hold you when you cry and say the things you need to hear to make you feel better—that is a rare find. Jonathan was my match.

But he also drove me nuts. Every shirt he owned had an ink stain on the pocket. When he ate, food erupted onto his tie or lap. He left the toilet seat up, piled dishes to Everest heights in the sink. His untidiness, his eating, his sentences that went on for days, punctuated by long pauses and *ums*, his chronic, incessant joking—all of this bothered me. And when I was bothered, I was expressive. Jonathan listened. He tried to change what he could. And then he broke up with me.

It broke my heart. But because of the care with which Jonathan ended our relationship, we were soon together again, this time as friends. Best friends.

Our friendship deepened and grew when, a few years after the romance had ended, we decided to co-parent Emma, a Vietnamese pot-bellied pig. Through the compromises and communication necessary for two people to properly raise a piglet, I learned to be more accepting and Jonathan was able to express his feelings to me.

Emma was a force of nature. She could open doors, cabinets,

childproof medicine bottles, zippers, bags, snaps, clips, and purses. She'd eat anything—except for onions, parsley, and celery. She once ate a box of green tea, including the bags, and was then so caffeinated that she bucked like a bronco and couldn't settle down for an entire night.

Emma mooed. She growled. She had a special gutteral "feed me" noise. When bored, Emma oinked incessantly, wagging her tail. When thinking, she was eerily still and silent. Silence from the pig was usually cause for alarm: Emma had no moral center. Like a dog, she knew when she was bad. Unlike a dog, she didn't care.

At the too-young age of three and a half, Emma passed away. Jonathan and I clung to each other, shattered. The strength of our loving friendship helped each of us through the loss.

I used to joke that animals disappoint you by dying, men by living. When you love critters whose life cycles are naturally much shorter than your own, you know that you will outlive the critter, if not the love. Your heart breaks more often than you think you can stand. And when you love a man, even the best of men, you take on having to see yourself, all your insecurities and inadequacies, and, if that's not enough to deal with, you also take on his.

We accept so much from our animals. We're not embarrassed if they eat sloppily; we don't cringe if they lick themselves in public. Humans, well, it's harder. Learning to forgive the faults of others—and ourselves—there's a task.

If an animal disappoints you, you have only yourself to blame: a lack of understanding, unrealistic expectations, unclear communications. Loving animals allows us to access the most tender, the most vulnerable, parts of ourselves. Their needs are relatively simple: food, water, a soft place to sleep, exercise, activities to keep their minds engaged, and love. Animals ask us to love them—it's our job to figure out how. And then they love us back.

It's not an either/or proposition, loving animals and loving men. We don't have to choose. (Unless, of course, he doesn't like animals, and then, well, clearly, he's not a good choice, at least not for people like me.)

But as we reach a certain age, it's harder to find men who are, in fact, a good fit. When you live only with a pet, it's hard to make the compromises necessary to allow another person into your intimate space. You don't want to have to train someone—especially as an adult—to put the toilet seat down or to wash his own dishes. And if you're out of a long relationship, getting used to the rhythms of your own life can be captivating—and hard to give up. When, as a spectator, I am privy to the inevitable spats and hissy fits of couples; when, as a weary traveler in the adult world, I get to sleep diagonally across my own bed; when I make plans to do exactly what I want to do, to go where I want to go—I relish my unpartnered state.

But I am not happy to come home to an empty apartment.

I am now single. I hope to find another man, a man I can love as unreservedly as I've loved my many pets, to whom I can extend the lessons of tolerance and patience I've learned from my critters. But even if I don't end up with a human partner, I know that I will not be alone. There are a lot of great animals out there.

CHARLIE'S AUNT

Diane Mapes

They came in twos starting around 6:30, their arms burdened with casserole dishes, salad fixings, diet pop, and car seats great with child. They were the graduating parents and successful class projects of a Babies 101 seminar; tonight was the long-awaited "baby reunion," where all participants got their chance to show and tell.

My sister, hostess of the event, had recruited me—her sole unfettered sibling—to help after her husband had invited everyone in a moment of magnanimous goodwill, brought on, no doubt, by pre-birth jitters. I didn't mind, really. After all, it meant I could hang out with my nephew Charlie, who loved me even though I knew far more about books than babies. And it gave me a chance to spend the evening with a group of women who thought *I* was in great shape. That alone made it worth the price of admission.

Nelly Mae was the first to arrive, stuffed into pink striped leg warmers like a miniature aerobics instructor. Raven-haired Mavis, named for her late grandmother, came soon thereafter, followed by roly-poly Alfred, taciturn Tavish, and, finally, quiet, contemplative Grace.

Coats were shrugged off, names were scrawled on tags and slapped onto jackets and sweaters and onesies, and soon the place filled with the jaunty air of a convention. "Hello, My Name Is Peggy's Sister," my name tag read. No point in delving into things further, I quickly realized, whisking a tin-foiled pork roast out to the kitchen. To this coupled-up crowd, I would never be anything more than the "unmarried sister." I might as well have written Mary Richards or Miss Jane or, perhaps, Rose Marie, of *Hollywood Squares* fame. We were all just spinsters, after all. Interchangeable, expendable, practically invisible.

As classmates chatted, I brought around drinks, stacked diaper bags next to the fireplace, and listened to a medley of "oohs" and "aahs" as each baby was unveiled. I oohed and aahed a bit myself. After all, the guests of honor were painfully cute, despite their ridiculously small baseball uniforms and soft pink bunny suits. Still in that questionably conscious stage, they stared at each other with baffled expressions as parents jostled them up and down, providing entertaining voiceovers.

"Just listen to that gas," a father boasted proudly to a smiling couple.

"Enjoy it while you can," I leaned over and whispered to the little fellow. "In ten years' time, you'll be in big trouble if you try that at one of your parents' parties."

Snacking on crackers and pesto cream cheese, the guests nonchalantly quizzed each other on a host of highly personal topics. Was it a vaginal delivery? How dilated was she when they gave her the epidural? Where were you when the water broke? I felt as if I'd accidentally stumbled into some strange parallel universe where the rules of propriety no longer applied. At any moment, a complete stranger might turn to me and ask if I cared to hear about his testicular abnormalities. Or wonder, perhaps, if my nipples felt a little sore and chafed. Someone mentioned the phrase *mucous plug*, and I fled to the kitchen to check on the lasagna.

Snatches of conversation wafted in as I sliced the French bread, tossed together salads, and distributed bottles of beer to the men. The women, the lot of them breast-feeders, stuck with caffeine-free juices.

"I hit her in the head with the phone the first week," one woman laughed nervously. "You should have heard the konk!"

"I dropped him in the middle of Babies R Us," a man said quietly. "Traumatized at least three fathers."

Other tales of terror and malfeasance followed, stories of wrenching bouts of diaper rash, malfunctioning baby monitors ("Ours picks up the neighbors' cordless phone; they're going to Mexico on vacation."), and uncontrollable milk-laden breasts ("I can squirt Kevin from clear across the room!"). With the arrival of the final guests, the babies were lined up eight across on the oversized sofa, and cameras began to flash with the intensity of a Hollywood premiere. A flurry of poses followed. Babies with mothers. Babies with fathers. Babies with bottles of beer. Then dinner was served.

Everyone ate in shifts, all struggling to juggle bottles of milk, bottles of ale, buckling plates, and bucking babies. I wolfed down some lasagna, salad, and a bit of crusty bread, then coaxed Charlie from my sister's hands and headed for the family room adjacent to the kitchen, where mothers had one by one retired to surreptitiously nurse by the soft light of a flickering TV.

There, the two of us snuggled in a comfortable overstuffed chair, he contently sucking down formula, me delighted that I finally got to spend some quality time with the only man currently in my life.

Unlike everyone else at the party, Charlie was oblivious to the fact that I was the sole single person there, the only woman without a child, or a husband, of my very own. Not that it bothered me at all. But I couldn't help but notice the sympathetic stares from some of the mothers as they glanced first at my bare ring finger and then at my name tag, perhaps expecting to find "Hello, My Name Is Single and Barren," scrawled in tear-spattered felt pen.

Charlie and I laughed at the idea like co-conspirators. As if *everybody's* cut out for marriage and motherhood, he seemed to whisper to me, affably filling his diaper. Exactly, I thought, hastening to find my sister.

As dinner wound down, I picked up stray dishes and, on my sister's suggestion, hauled chairs into the crowded living room so all the parties could gather in a lopsided circle to share delivery stories. Even from the kitchen, I could hear a change in tone as the voices quieted and the birthing order was determined. Suddenly, I felt as if I were six years old again, sitting around a roaring campfire, swapping scary stories with a group of wide-eyed neighbor kids. The yarns these adults shared rivaled even those gruesome childhood favorites like The Hook, The Hand, and Bloody Bones and the Butcher Knife.

Julie had endured labor for twenty-two hours when the baby's heart rate suddenly dropped and they had to "open her up." Jack saw his child's head suddenly appear "as big as a beach ball and so greasy the doctors couldn't even grab it." While the men talked of wading through piles of bloody rags on operating room floors and of doctors in farm boots so they could "at least keep their feet dry," the women whispered of botched spinal injections, excruciating labor, and cords wrapped tight around gasping babies' necks.

I was just happy that the clatter of dishes and splashing water drowned out half of the unrelenting stories of pain, pressure, and poor television reception. *You feel sorry for me?* I wanted to shout at the women who'd given me sympathetic looks earlier in the evening. *Hey, I'm not the one who had to be sewn back up like a Thanksgiving turkey.*

Coffee and dessert followed, and shortly thereafter, couples began to drift toward the door, babies in tow. Binkies were found, bottles retrieved, forgotten toys quickly tossed from the front porch into outstretched, overtaxed arms.

I picked up coffee cups and bottle caps, plastic forks and half-eaten meals, plates abandoned for a damp diaper, a hungry wail. The nibbled sandwiches and forsaken wedges of pie seemed a clear indicator of the shape of things to come, but none of the parents seemed to mind. Truly, who could begrudge a miracle?

Out the door went Mavis, the tiny girl with the grown-up name; Zachary, obviously destined for the major leagues; cranky, colicky Callie, her bleary-eyed parents already discussing the night's sleep strategies. A lone couple lingered at the door with my sister and her husband, their conversations nervously flitting from the price of formula to the promise of swimming lessons to the dreaded specter of thrush.

Charlie was settled comfortably in my arms, his eyes nearly as wide as those of the adults who had attended tonight's gala event. I listened to the tone of sheer wonder that permeated the parents' conversation. I smelled Charlie's sweet, soft innocence, wondering if that slight twinge I felt deep inside was regret or something else. Obviously, it was too late in the game to take this path myself. Not only was I over forty, but I was single and happily so. Sure, there were other ways of going about having a baby on your own, if having a baby were the end-all, be-all. But it had never seemed the right route for me. And I knew it never would be. Call it selfish or maybe just self-aware, but as long as I had no children of my own, I could stay one myself in perpetuity. And that seemed to suit me just fine.

Was that such a bad thing? I wondered. Was I somehow less a woman, some odd poseur in panty shields, just because I hadn't given birth myself? Just because I couldn't contribute my *own* mucous-plug tale at some Tupperware party of the future? Did *every* woman have to be a mom? Or were there acceptable alternatives? I thought about my own childhood, surrounded by quarrelsome sisters, nurturing grandmothers, conspiratorial aunts. It almost seemed as if I'd made my decision years ago, perhaps the first time my great aunt Florence had suggested we rubberband a paper towel around one of our cat's hind legs. I'd been about five years old at the time, Florence probably fifty-five, and the two of us had nearly peed our pants laughing. I was laughing still.

Charlie wriggled in my arms, clunked his head against mine, buckled and burbled and laughed a bit himself. Oh, get over yourself, I thought I heard him whisper conspiratorially. As if just *anybody's* cut out to be an aunt.

A New Leash on Life

Patti Lawson

I was sitting on the couch with my dream date—a handsome, successful banker I'd met by chance. After a long, lingering lunch, I felt it was time to bring him home. He was saying sweet everythings: "You are so pretty . . . so soft . . . oh yes, Sadie girl . . . you're just perfect." Unfortunately, my name was not Sadie and he was not saying them to me. Sadie is my dog. She'd endeared herself to my Prince Charming as I sat watching. One of the many dilemmas I was to encounter since I'd begun dating again.

This guy passed the litmus test I'd devised before cautiously beginning my dating odyssey. His behavior with her when I was out of the room was impeccable. He'd gotten down on the floor to play with her; he'd petted her and let her lick his face. Most importantly, I heard him tell her: "I really like your mom." What Sadie and I were soon to discover was that he liked the moms of lots of other dogs, too.

After years of living alone and then going through a longterm relationship, I was dating and I had a dog—two things I never imagined I'd be doing at this age. After giving up on men and love and even life, I'd been transformed by a most unexpected agent: a little homeless dog who, among other things, showed me that it was never too late for anything and that I could learn to love again. It had begun with an ending.

In his poem "Dover Beach," Matthew Arnold looked out over the cliffs of Dover on a moonlit night and lamented that the world had "neither joy, nor love, nor light, nor certitude, nor peace, nor help for pain." In a former life as a student and a teacher of literature, I'd been in awe of such groupings of words and at the mystery of the underlying emotions that had enabled the writer to create them. Now as a fortysomething lawyer, with a mortgage and way too much time out of the cloistered walls of academia, I loathed not only the fact that these words existed, but also that I'd ever had the misfortune to read them, much less to know firsthand what they meant. Now, I knew what awful anguish gives someone the skill to string thoughts and words such as these together. A romance that I'd been certain would *last* a lifetime had in one day become the romance *of* a lifetime, and it was over.

While I, like most other women who make it to what is called midlife, had experienced my share of heartbreak, this was profoundly different. I felt washed up, alone on the scary shore of solitude. And this time, I felt it was forever. The youthful elasticity that had enabled me to bounce back from previous relationships was gone. I felt paralyzed by emptiness and unable to feel anything except that my insides were crumbled into a million little pieces and I had no idea how I'd ever feel whole again, or whether I even wanted to.

I soon discovered that I was not alone in my vulnerability by talking to other women my age and older who'd loved and lost this late in life. There was a pervasive consensus that it was harder to recover from a lost love in the over-forty bracket; we simply didn't have as much time ahead of us as we once had. Women whose husbands had walked out after twenty or even thirty years and women who had lost a boyfriend all felt the same. The reasons for the breakups were much like mine: a mixture of clichéd excuses but, in the end, irrelevant. I was living Bonnie Raitt's song—I'd become that woman her soulful voice portrayed: "She's scared . . . scared she'll run out of time."

I'd known the man I'd lost a very long time. He'd shared ten years with me and had made it possible for me to ignore the changes year after year because he always found me beautiful— still young at heart and in body. But he was gone, and so was my confidence in my ability to ever find someone else.

Except for minor musings, this was only the second time that the prospect of being older and alone hit me full force. The first had occurred right after I'd bought my house.

I'd been ecstatic when I bought the house. I'd arrived in Charleston, West Virginia, five years before, with a new law degree, an old convertible stuffed with everything I owned, and some worn furniture hardly worth the storage fees I'd paid to keep it until I could afford an apartment. I'd traded an unfulfilling marriage for three years of law school and never looked back.

I'd taken a low-paying job as a government staff attorney, then started my own practice on the side, and here I was: the first woman in my family to ever buy a house on her own. I was overjoyed to have proven wrong my ex-husband's dire predictions that I'd have nothing without him. Here was tangible proof of how wrong he'd been: a three-story colonial within walking distance of my job . . . and it was all mine.

When my renovations were completed, I walked through the beautifully colored rooms as my shoes echoed loudly on the refinished hardwood floors. The glow from the new light fixtures landed on the newly painted walls, giving them a serene quality not seen in their vibrant daytime mode. I lit the gas fireplaces and walked through each and every room admiring the transformation. I ran my hand over the shiny new washer and dryer; no more coin-laundry machines in the basement of my apartment building for me. From the basement to the third floor I took in the splendor of my "new" seventy-year-old house.

And then it happened. I looked in the mirror of the master bathroom, and it hit me. I was going to be walking through these same rooms and I would be looking in the same mirror when I was old. Would I be able to climb the steps to the third floor? As I stared at my face in the bathroom mirror, examining every feature, my eyes filled with tears, and at a moment when I had every reason to rejoice, I began to cry.

But I'd survived that emotional crisis and had spent the last seven years enjoying my role as a homeowner and my career as a lawyer. I'd done well enough to have a couple of Armani suits and a Mercedes convertible. I'd taken some fantastic vacations and been generous with my family. I planted roses and herbs and built my own patio. My house was the center of happy times with family and friends—and the man who was now gone.

I'd met him all those years ago when he rescued my car from the rain. I'd left the top down, and he knocked on my door and asked for the keys to put it up. And of all the houses I could've bought, this house was across the street from where he lived—where we'd met that long-ago summer. The arrangement was like living in a very big house with a street in the middle of it. Our trips back and forth across the street were endless. But now, but now the distance across the street seemed as vast as an ocean, and I was helpless to swim across it.

Was I getting paid back for all the times I'd skirted the issue of commitment and walked away from men who had wanted to take care of me? In all the partnerships I'd had with men over the years, I'd always reserved a part of me that they couldn't have. Was there someone at some point along the way I should have stayed with?

Time passed, and when I'd eaten enough Godiva to raise the stock price a few points, gained enough weight to move up a size (or two), I remembered something more important than a lost love. Some of my most wonderful memories were those with my horse Misty. I'd take a book and an egg salad sandwich and escape the continual din of a house filled with my numerous siblings. During those tranquil afternoons, I developed a real appreciation for solitude and the freedom I felt galloping over the fields to my hideaway. Not only did my early love for books begin there, so did my ability to connect with another living creature on a deep level. Slowly, the answer came to me: of course I couldn't have a horse in my backyard, but what about a dog?

Life-changing trips are supposed to take place in India or Europe or the mountains. Not so for me. On a cold, sunny March day, I drove to PetsMart, and it changed my life. There in the pen where puppies sit waiting to be adopted, I found my soul mate. I'd walked into the store just to look, and before I knew it, I was on the way back home with a little black dog in the back seat of my convertible.

My expectations of what this dog could do for me were ambiguous at best, but at least I wouldn't be the only living being in my lonely house anymore. Ours was not a love at first sight. First of all, I played the dance-away lover with her as I had with most of the men in my past. I took her back. I find it unthinkable now, but I did. She barked all night that first night, and although I'd been ruing the tomblike quiet of my house, this dog din was not what I considered an improvement.

Without her, the silence was worse than before, and in one night, the flashes of memory in that big empty house weren't about the man I'd lost, but of the cute little dog that needed a home.

I wasn't sure this would work, but I was willing to give it a try. Moping on the couch for months, eating, and cloistering myself off from the world certainly hadn't helped, and maybe this little dog could bring back some of those feelings I'd discovered with Misty. And if not, I couldn't see how it could possibly make anything worse.

I was wrong. Everything was worse in the beginning. I never knew when to feed her or when to take her out. She wailed when I left her to go to work; she barked when I wanted to sleep or talk on the phone. I'd have to rush home to get her out at lunch time and go straight home after work to care for her. Between feedings, baths, walks, and nocturnal bathroom trips outside, I was worn out. I was operating on autopilot, but I wasn't crying myself to sleep anymore or eating my way through the refrigerator contents every other night. But through it all, we maintained an aloofness from each other that was beginning to make me think. She had a confidence about her that I admired, going about her daily life independently, not showing one sign of longing for anything she'd left behind.

And then one day I got a call at my office. The lady from the adoption organization had a lot of questions about the dog and her health. I was speechless as I listened. This dog had been exposed to some disease that had killed all the other puppies she'd lived with. I needed to watch her closely, and if she started showing any of the signs that had just been described to me, I'd have to take her to the vet.

All of a sudden all the images of this dog that had been swallowed up in feedings, bathroom trips, early risings, barking, and begging came dancing before my eyes. Her joyful spirit each morning. Her cautious regarding of me, almost sensing that this tenuous arrangement between us might not be permanent.

The delicate way she took her treats and the equally quick snap of her mouth when she crunched an ice cube. How she stood on her hind legs and twirled around in the kitchen, happy to see her breakfast. How she gobbled her food so quickly and then wanted mine. How she never missed the smell of anything remotely signifying food and came running at the sound of the refrigerator. The way she dashed up the basement steps and then ran back to peek down as if to hurry me up. The little teeth marks in all my tulips and the chews scattered around the house. The towel on the back porch to dry her paws off with, and the way she looked when she was wet from her bath.

Suddenly, it was all dear to me. I was no longer greeted by silence when I opened the door. My house had gone from clean to comfortable, and I'd hardly noticed. Her possessions and mine alike were scattered around together in domestic familiarity. When I wasn't looking, an eight-pound antidepressant on four legs had taken over my house. But more than the physical changes in the house, I had changed. It wasn't all about me anymore.

I hung up the phone and ran the two blocks from my office to my house in very high heels. I realized as I ran home that this dog needed me and I needed her. I threw open the front door and ran to the basement where she was clinging to the door of her crate and yelled, "Mom is home!" I opened the door, and when she jumped up, I caught her. I held her close and I began crying harder than I could ever remember. I wasn't crying for what I'd lost or because I was getting older or because I was alone. I was crying because I found something I'd thought was gone forever: I had learned to love again.

That day was almost two years ago, and that dog became Sadie, my roommate, my confidant, and the wisest teacher I've ever had. My days start with a smile as I open my eyes and hear her high-speed tail thumping the mattress as our eyes make contact. She's taken over a shelf in my office, the passenger seat in my car, and a large portion of my heart. On that day when I held her close and cried grateful and healing tears, we created an unshakable bond.

One day Sadie will be older than me. On this timetable of life, she'll accelerate and pass my chronological age; that's just the way it goes. One day Sadie was a very small puppy nipping the hem of my bathrobe, and the next day she was a skinny long-legged dog following me around. One day I was a carefree girl with lots of romances behind and before me—and one day I became a woman on her own. But I've come to love the age I am, and the years that have passed, because they bring freedom and wisdom along with them. I've grown comfortable in my own skin (with or without concealer or wrinkles) and my own time.

I'm thankful that my heart was broken. It gave me time to discover things I might never have known and made enough room for Sadie to run in. She made me see that there was room for someone else there as well—maybe a dad for her?

And so, Sadie and I started dating again, thus the afternoon with the handsome banker. I was able to bid him adieu without any remorse and no thoughts at all that he was perhaps the "last chance." Sadie and I revel in our singleness together, taking time to carefully evaluate the men who go through our screening process.

But both of us have that ever-hopeful attitude and know that it has nothing in common with "always longing." Sadie and I take long walks and just enjoy the moment. We get quite a bit of attention from men, but for now we're just enjoying each other and giving those squirrels on the Capitol lawn a run for their lives. However, we're keeping our unlimited options open. You never know what's around the next corner—or even just across the street.

House of Hormones

Susan Maushart

It has become an article of faith among adult people today that "you're only as young as you feel." As a single mother of three school-age children, I can only say, "Oh God, I hope not."

Like every other female baby boomer on the planet, I object to the term *middle-aged*. *Midlife* is different somehow. It is softer and more flattering, a pearlescent forty-watt lightbulb of a word. And yet I am old enough to remember a time when *midlife* was a term that belonged exclusively to men. (Remember the midlife crisis? It used to be something only guys got—like jock itch, or promotion to partner.)

I accept that I am at midlife, albeit in the same way that I accept collect calls from my fourteen-year-old—that is, grudgingly. But most of the time, I am as much in denial about how old I really am as any other member of my generation. ("You're only young once, but you can stay immature indefinitely," a large fridge magnet reminds me, encouragingly.) Six days a week, I still wear blue jeans and thongs—the old-fashioned kind that separate only your toes. And my daughters are constantly begging me to wear more makeup and accessories, exactly as my mother did back in the '70s.

I tell my kids the good part about growing up is how much

you don't change on the inside, where it really counts. I try not to think about my pelvic floor when I say this.

Like the old gray mare—and, really, she *could* have had a few foils done—midlife ain't what it used to be. When my mother, who is seventy-three, was my age, which is forty-seven, she was already an empty nester. She'd had her babies much, much younger—and we returned the favor by fledging much, much earlier. OK, partly it was her blender chop suey. But partly it was just what young people did in those days. They *moved out.*

Remember moving out? It was what you used to do when you wanted to have sex. Now kids have sex in their bedrooms, right among the teddy bears. "Better they should do it safely at home than in a parked car somewhere," my friends with older teenagers rationalize. That's true, I guess. Yet I can't help thinking: you have the whole rest of your life to have sex safely at home. Whereas doing it in a parked car has a definite shelf life. But I think I'm getting off the topic, don't you?

At forty-seven, my own children are aged ten, twelve, and fourteen—and that's about as far from an empty nest as you can get without a doctor's prescription. For those women who embarked on motherhood in their twenties (which seems like such a good idea, all of a sudden), I suspect midlife has a different texture—and a much, much quieter soundtrack. For those who have remained "child-free"—a mere generation ago, the preferred term was *barren*—I imagine midlife to have a more seamless quality. Then again, perhaps not. Perhaps, in the absence of offspring, such women experience an added urgency to become fully who they are.

But what about women who, like me, find themselves in midlife at the very epicenter of family life—and going it solo besides? We will devote our midlife years to arguably the most demanding and certainly the most mentally taxing phase of our parenting lives. Heaven knows, we don't have time for a "crisis."

Hell, we barely have time to floss. When I think of the thousands I'm saving on therapy, this doesn't seem like a bad bargain. And yet, to be still gunning the engine at a time when your body is longing to be set to cruise control is, I suspect, a mixed blessing. I know for sure it's a consequence of the decision to delay motherhood that I never, ever conceived of.

We can repeat the mantra that "fifty is the new thirty" all we like. And trust me, I do like. Yet women who become mature-age mothers by choice—and then end up single by circumstance—do not magically collect an extra two decades for their daring. On the contrary. There are many, many Monday mornings when fifty feels more like the new sixty-five: high time a sensible person retired down South and devoted herself to extreme leisure—collecting rare elderly suitors, say, or knitting frequent-flier points for the grandkids.

I have been officially perimenopausal for about three years now, dating it generally from the time my periods started going haywire and specifically from the night I bled through two super-plus tampons and a pad thicker than a Huggies nighttime disposable while onstage performing in *The Vagina Monologues*. I also have a teenage daughter, as I mentioned, and two "tweens" rapidly coming up the queue. Sometimes there are so many hormones in the atmosphere I swear you can see them, hanging over our house like some toxic mist. "Please, God, don't let us all transform at once," I find myself praying. "The TV room isn't big enough."

As what you might call a career solo parent—having been on my own since my kids were four, two, and barely sitting up—I've had ample opportunity to observe that necessity really *is* the single mother of invention. And self-reliance is the sperm donor. Simply put, being a single parent forces you to do things differently because you have to. Sometimes it's the small stuff—the sweating of which is every mother's basic job description.

Occasionally, it's the XXL stuff. Cumulatively, those differences add up to a family culture both distinctive (OK, weird) and surprisingly sturdy.

When there were three under five, in as many rooms, I bathed them together every night and washed their hair, assembly-line fashion, every night, too. It was easier that way. And you knew for sure where everybody was. If I'd had more leisure and more help—or a smaller bathtub—I doubt I would have made that choice. Yet that nightly ritual taught us all so many useful life skills. How to take turns, for example. How to have fun in a very, very small space. How to holler when you noticed the water closing over somebody's head. I used to be proud of the way my kids "got on" with each other (as we say in Australia). Now I realize that a big part of it was that we simply *had* to "get on"—or the water would have closed over all of our heads.

As a mother, you have only one mind and one body, and a child will consume 100 percent of each of them. So will three children. You can't give more than everything, so they learn to be content with smaller pieces. And so do you, really. With no partner to pass the buck to—or to come home and stake out an interval called "adult time"—you learn how to live *with* your kids, not around them or in spite of them.

Tolstoy was wrong about family life. All happy families are *not* happy in the same way—and we are living proof of that. There are a thousand ways to get it right. And many of them contradict absolutely the received wisdom we have learned, as Parents Who Think Too Much, to recite by rote. One of my own secret maternal weapons, I realize more and more, is how much I don't do for my children—not because I don't want to, but simply because I can't.

My kids are not overindulged with lessons and sport and "enrichment," as if they were so many loaves of mixed-grain bread. The reason is partly financial. Partly it's philosophical (busyness, I have always believed, is the last refuge of the unimaginative). But mostly it's pragmatic. Unlike Stephen Leacock's horseman, who leapt on his steed and galloped off in all directions, I drive a Subaru. And, alas, it can only go one place at a time. Around here, decisions about extracurricular commitments are of necessity *family* matters. (So, too, is extensive knowledge of the public transit system.) With only one adult at the helm, our family has never known the luxury of being exclusively child-centered. Or the curse.

Unlike many of my partnered girlfriends, I never agonized about co-sleeping with my young children. Perhaps that's ironic, given that I was the one with the extra legroom. (Another joy of single life too rarely celebrated: sleeping starfished smack-dab in the middle of a queen-size bed.) But the fact was, I needed my sleep and my space. Every inch of it. I regret that my needs made me hard-hearted at times. But somebody was going to have to do some controlled crying, and I was damned if it was going to be me. I'd done enough of that in my marriage.

Being a single parent teaches you that children are a bit like bougainvillea. A little benign neglect, and the occasional ruthless cutting back, can work wonders. The problem is, I am a hopeless gardener, so it's a lesson I am prone to forget. As a mother, it is so easy to recede—so tempting, at times, to dwindle to two dimensions, to lose hold of who you are and (as a professor of mine used to say) what you represent. And that goes double when you are a single mother, and double again when you hit midlife at full throttle, with three hormonally challenged passengers whooping it up in the back seat. If I had a partner, I sometimes think, I'd least I'd have someone to *blame*. But in my more lucid intervals, I recognize that the road I'm on—though a long way from the route I'd planned on—has led me to places I'd never have gotten to otherwise. And the truth is, I prefer a bumpy ride. At least you know you're moving.

NUDE AWAKENING

Cameron Tuttle

I am sitting on a plane between Oakland and Burbank enjoying the in-flight beverage service when I notice a lovely, delicate pattern of wrinkles in the blue pleather seatback in front of me. Then it hits me—I am *single* again, and I am . . . Wait, how old am I? I've been lying about my age for so long that even my brother can't remember how old he really is. Oh, shit. I remember. This being single again is going to be worse than I thought.

It's not that I didn't want this relationship to end. I did. It was time. It was my idea. Honest. But I wanted it to end when I was, I don't know, younger and cuter and firmer and not insanely stressed. I didn't plan this very well. Can I even get naked with a stranger at my age? I don't know.

I bite at the edge of the little bag of peanuts and try to imagine my fabulous new single life. There I am, looking rested and hot. I am surrounded by witty, attractive, age-appropriate urban hipsters, everyone exchanging politically informed yet playful banter. Mouths open, heads tossed back in laughter. Someone refills my Riedel glass with red wine, probably a Rhone blend; then I raise it and propose a toast, "To old body parts, new friends, and new exp—" I stop and take a good look around the room.

Who *are* these people? I never recognize anyone in my fabulous-life fantasies. I don't even recognize myself anymore. I never look that rested. Why do I always look so tired?

Suddenly, I get that nervous pins-and-needles feeling. I'm not just single, I am alone. I am profoundly and deeply alone. Alone in my crowded fabulous-life fantasies. Alone on this crowded plane. Alone in Hollywood, where I'll be living for the next five months in a furnished corporate apartment. They are turning my books into a TV show. *They* are a studio, a network, and a small snake pit of producers I don't trust and writers I don't get. I'll be painfully alone in my lack of appreciation for jokes about poop, big boobs, and drunken sluts. They are turning my books into a TV show! I should be happy. I should be ecstatic. I am one of the lucky ones. I am living the dream, baby! Air kisses.

I take a swig of club soda and swallow hard. I want to cry. But I can't. I'm sitting in a middle seat. Everyone knows you're not allowed to cry in a middle seat. It's part of the social contract of low-fare travel. In a middle seat, you must keep your elbows and your emotions in. That's the deal. Besides, I wouldn't want to make Steve and Eric feel uncomfortable.

Steve and Eric are nice, normal guys, guys who cheerfully offer to hold your coffee when you're struggling to wedge into the middle seat, panting and sweating from an unscheduled sprint to the gate, guys who go to real estate conferences on weekends just for fun, guys who look genuinely happy to be wearing pressed khakis and almost-matching polo shirts. Steve and Eric even smell nice. And they both have big, strong shoulders, perfect for a girl to cry on.

God, I wish I could call my mom and tell her how alone and how scared I feel. But I can't do that either.

Instead, I pretend to read the nutritional stats on the tiny peanut bag as I casually lift the bottom edge of my shirt and slip a roasted peanut into my belly button. It goes in easy. Once, in my twenties, I found a popcorn kernel in my belly button. The best part—I hadn't been to the movies in over a week. At the time, I thought that was hilarious, especially because I was showering every day and having torrid, sweaty sex every night. But if that happened now, it would be sad, really sad.

I finger a few more peanuts from the bag, pop one in my mouth, and crunch down hard. I can't let Steve and Eric see this. Jeez, I don't want them to think I'm some kind of weirdo. Then, ever so discreetly, I ease a second peanut into my belly button. Damn. It fits. Now I feel alone and scared and depressed. Middle age has renovated my once-enviable tight little innie into a two-peanut garage.

Can I get naked with a stranger at my age? Should I? I don't know.

I close my eyes and try to picture it. The lights are low (of course); a candle flickers on the bedside table. Soft, sexy, love-bumpin' music plays in my mind. There I am, emotionally and physically naked, sprawled seductively across high-thread-count sheets, awaiting a dark and mysterious hottie's entrance into my love lair. Wait, wait, wait. Where is my body? What is that blob? Turn up the lights. My body is one big blurry blob, and not Vaseline-gauzy blurry—more like pixilated, someone-committed-a-crime blurry. My eyes pop open. I realize, trying to suppress both disbelief and disgust, that I have no idea what my naked body looks like now.

Well, I have been busy, very busy actually, for the past few years. I tap, tap, tap the bag of peanuts, emptying crumbs into my mouth, then carefully fold it into a perfect little foil square. I drop it into the beverage cup on the tray table and watch it expand. But it's not like I never look at my nude body. Come on, I soap and scrub and examine my skin for clogged pores. You bet, I shave and wax and pluck. Of course, I exfoliate and moisturize and apply sunscreen. Who doesn't?

But have I spent any quality time with my body? No. I can't remember the last time I luxuriated in my nakedness. I haven't caressed or traced or worshipped or explored in ages. Oh, God. It's worse than that. I have been treating my body like a dolly, a piece of equipment to transport my mouth and my brain to and from work. This is not good. This will not play well at cocktail parties. No one wants to have sex with a dolly.

I vow to make a searching and fearless moral inventory of my bod when I get to Burbank. I will introduce myself to folds and flaps. I will network with my nooks and cranny. I will celebrate my cellulite. I will meet and greet every glorious sag and curve. I will love myself up and fall hard for my soft body. I will get naked with a stranger tonight, and that stranger will be me.

Steve pokes his finger into my shoulder. "Sigourney Weaver!" he says with gusto. "That's who you look like."

"I do?" I ask, trying for a natural blend of graciousness and surprise. "Thanks, Steve."

"I bet you hear that all the time," says Eric, nodding with a knowing smile.

"I do," I admit. "But I never get tired of hearing it."

"You could totally be her sister," adds Steve.

Her what? I am like a million years younger than she is. I could be her illegitimate daughter from a high school fling.

"Thank you," I say cheerfully. "Really nice talking with you guys."

As I head off the plane, I make a mental note: Remove Sigourney Weaver mention from online profile.

I drop my bags at my temporary apartment, which looks more like a Macy's furniture showroom than anyone's home. I've given myself a day to get settled, reacclimate, and brace myself for months of Hollywood hell.

My first stop is the gym, or rather a chic health club I foolishly joined as a way to maintain my sanity during the months of production. It seemed like a good idea at the time. But that was before I visited the women's locker room, which is painted a fashionable and soothing celadon and scented with organic lavender. Los Angeles bodies are noticeably different from San Francisco bodies.

I sneak a few peeks at the women around me while slowly peeling off my layers, a combo plate of last year's Banana Republic and a few overpriced boutique items that I am probably too old and too white to be wearing. Wow. Is everyone spray-tanning but me? All of the women in here look absolutely flawless. Brazilians are back. Or maybe they never left. I am so out of it. I'm going to drown in the dating pool. The drag of my body hair alone will pull me under. I quickly wrap a towel around my pale self and take a long, lingering sip from my electrolyte-infused water. Amazing. Every woman, regardless of shape, age, or height, has exactly the same boobs. The sheer tonnage of silicone implants in this room is enough to make the most secure "natural" girl feel not just inadequate but inhuman.

I am starting to feel tired, very tired. I turn to catch my reflection in one of the many mirrors. Oh yeah, very tired. In fact, I look exhausted. Maybe I shouldn't actually work out today. It might be a shock to my system. Just showing up at the gym and undressing is enough to get my heart rate up. I decide to hit the steam room to detox and relax before my big "me" date tonight.

Oh look. There's a woman with real breasts. And I recognize her. She's an actress on that popular one-hour drama. Very cool, very impressive, she has real breasts. And she's gorgeous, even more beautiful in person than she is on TV. And she's following me to the steam room. I have to pull hard on the door to break the heat lock. As I open the door, a peanut hits the tile floor and rolls toward a drain.

The actress and her size-zero friend stretch out on the top shelf. I settle in on the lower level. I know my place. A blast of eucalyptus steam fills the air. I close my eyes and try to relax, but the actress and her friend won't shut up.

"You're too skinny now," whines size zero.

"I am not," says the actress. "I just did a juice fast while on holiday."

Is that a fake British accent?

"Too skinny. Yes, you are. I'm worried about you."

"No. I am so not too skinny. You're just jealous."

OK, I am out of here. This is not cool, not impressive, not relaxing, and not helping me prepare for my body-loving date with myself. What if I can't handle the pressure of living in L.A.? What if I freak out after a few months and blow my TV loot on personal development instead of putting it into a SEP IRA? I imagine myself returning home to San Francisco as a blonde with swollen, kissable lips, a lifted and Botoxed brow, and huge knockers. I step out of the cab, all tanned legs and fabulous designer pumps. I drop my bags, open the front door, and make my entrance. My cat takes one look at me and hisses.

When I return home to my furniture showroom, nothing hisses at me. It is dead space. Even the plants are plastic. I click my iPod mini into the dock between two tiny speakers and hit the makeout mix. Maybe I can fill this place with some life. Maybe I can set the mood.

It's still light out, but I am determined. I take off my clothes and slip into a robe, as if that will add some allure to my unveiling. I have decided on a few basic ground rules:

1. Remain judgment-free for sixty seconds.

2. Be kind as well as fearless.

3. Drink some wine.

It's not that I need a drink to look at myself naked. It's just that, for best results, this should simulate a real date, right?

I step in front of the mirrored closet door, take a couple of deep breaths and a long sip of wine, a crisp, refreshing sauvignon blanc. Then I look down at my feet and let the robe fall to the floor. It's very dramatic. But I feel like a horny housewife in a bad porn movie.

I can't look up. Am I shy? Embarrassed? Nervous? Afraid?

My feet look fabulous, by the way. God bless the fourteen-dollar pedicure. I shift my weight from foot to foot, not quite dancing but hoping to groove my way into date mode. I take another sip of wine and slowly look up at my reflection. Swaying to a sultry Aaliyah tune, I gaze upon my full-length naked body. Wow. There is more of me than I remember.

One thousand one, one thousand two, one thousand three.

I have never had body issues. Really. I wonder if that means something is wrong with me. Am I unfeminine? Am I un-American? Maybe I am just a late bloomer. I've always cared about my body, but I've never cared enough to hate it. Besides, I was athletic and blessed with a very fast metabolism, which seemed to me a fair exchange for my very slow internal clock.

I could never understand why most girls were constantly comparing themselves to one another, striving and starving for perfection. It would never occur to me to compare myself to some movie star's body or to a model in a magazine. That would be stupid. A perfect body type is nothing but a collective typo—I know that. Yet here I am desperately fighting the urge to compare my "now" body to someone else's "wow" body.

What is my problem? What is this young, slender, tan, taut body doing in my head? I focus hard on my knees, trying to intimidate this image out of my brain. My knees are freckled. My knees are freckled and wrinkled?

Thirty-two, thirty-three, thirty-four. It's back. The hard, flat stomach, the shapely, fit yet feminine thighs. No, go away. Get out. I am on a me date! I close my eyes, feeling frustrated and pathetic. Damn it. Where is this coming from?

Oh? Oh, right. Oh, of course. It's that body from *that* summer.

I wonder if every woman keeps an image in her mind of how her body should look. I think so. But it's not a picture of a swimsuit model or Miss America or a Playboy playmate. It's a memory, an image file of an ideal body, your ideal body. It's the way you looked at your best or the way you thought you looked. It could be an actual snapshot you cherished and tucked away in a journal. Or maybe it's a mental shot you framed in the back of your mind and have developed again and again to keep it from fading. It might be the way you looked at camp in that paisley bikini the summer your breasts finally made you popular with the boys. It might be the time you backpacked around Greece with your best friend, wearing the same stinky halter top and short, short cutoffs, too poor to eat more than one meal a day. It might be the way you looked on your wedding day or on your twenty-fifth birthday or standing on the top of Half Dome buck naked in your hiking boots. Or maybe it was the way you looked very briefly after you had had mono for three months, took all those photos, and decided to become a model. Or it was the first time a boyfriend or a girlfriend loved you madly, adoring and praising every inch of you, and you finally believed that your body was perfect exactly as it was.

I was twenty-three, living at home, struggling to find my way after college, struggling to figure out how even to try to be a writer. During the day, I worked in a menial, mindless job and in the warm summer evenings trained for a triathlon. Swimming, running, and cycling had added a layer of cute girl muscles and carved away what little body fat I had. I was in the best shape of my life and I was in love, deep-crazy-obsessive love. I had fallen in love once before, but this was different, exciting, and dangerous. On the weekends, I would float around on a thick foam pad in the neighbor's pool, perfecting my tan while praying that some life plan would come to me before I lost my mind. I called myself The Graduette. It was that kind of summer, terrifying and confusing, thrilling and disillusioning. But my body, no matter how hard I pushed it, never let me down. That body is my perfect body.

Fifty-seven, fifty-eight, fifty-nine. . .

I have an awakening, a nude awakening. This is easy, I realize. All I have to do is update my mental files. That's it. Delete, purge, force quit, whatever it takes to replace my old body image with current raw data.

So I turn back to the mirror to continue my inventory. My thighs are long and pale with absolutely no visible sign of muscle tone. Where have I seen this body before? My shoulders are smaller and round, as if whatever muscle I once had has slipped off my shoulders and settled in my upper arms. Gravity is not my friend. What is that? What the hell was I stretching to get stretch marks there? My knees may be freckled and wrinkled, but I still have my collarbone, damn it, and a tastefully sun-damaged décolletage. I know I have seen this body somewhere before and definitely not at a gym.

Oh, my God, I have breasts! And they actually look damn good, finally. No longer a pudding cup, I am now a legitimate, better-use-two-hands B cup. I nod and smile proudly. And my droopage is perfectly symmetrical. That has got to be a sign of good genes, right? Or is it just good lingerie? My stomach looks a little soft, but I still have a waist. I turn to the side, appreciating my curvy if slightly sagging profile. There is more of me. But it's not bad; it's just different. I have shape. I have a real woman's body. I certainly don't need to lose any weight. Maybe I just need to reorganize it.

I reach for a couple of business cards from a messy pile on top of the dresser and tuck one under each breast. I can't help myself. They hold, even when I dance. Moving with the soulful, steady base beat, I turn around and around, admiring myself in the mirror. I dance over to the bathroom counter and grab a lip liner and an eyebrow pencil. I tuck one under each butt cheek. If I take baby steps, they hold, too. I love my new middle-aged body! I may never have to carry a purse again.

I dance back over to the mirror, laughing at the absurdity of my fears. And I have hips now, too. They are kind of low-rise hips, but they are hips. My mother used to call them saddlebags. For as long as I can remember, she was trying to drop the same ten pounds and lose her saddlebags.

Slowly, I stop dancing.

That is where I have seen this body before. This is my mother's body. The soft shoulders, the long legs, the pale skin, the. . . My mother was forty the last time I saw her body, actually, the last time anyone saw her body. I can remember her standing nude in the master bathroom after a shower, a radiation burn across the left side of her chest where her breast had been. She was joking with me about the indelible beet-red lines, dashes, and X's on her chest, guides for the radiologist. She called it her pirate's treasure map. I laughed with her, but I could not take my eyes off her heart, beating, beating, beating, through the paper-thin skin stretched over her ribs.

I smile and laugh again, knowing that she is laughing with me right now. I may not be young or tan or taut, but I am here. And I am not alone. I have a lifetime of good and bad dates ahead of me, I have a sense of humor, and I have all of my original parts. I am one of the lucky ones. I am living the dream. As long as I never date anyone who knew me naked twenty years ago, I am one hot, jiggly, wiggly middle-aged babe.

I raise my glass and propose a toast, "To old body parts, new friends, and new experiences."

I never saw that second peanut again. Maybe it fell out of my belly button when I was running to catch the airport shuttle. Or maybe it washed away in the shower with my fears of being single at this age. Or maybe it was never there at all.

Acknowledgments

To Karen Bouris, for not taking no for an answer, for pushing me beyond what I thought I was capable of doing, and for being so kind and helpful. You are a dream publisher. Drinks in Maui on me.

To Autumn Stephens, for talking me down out of the trees when I wondered why this writer was attempting to be an editor.

To the twenty-eight fabulous authors who join me in this anthology: for taking this assignment so seriously, for being so gracious with my requests for changes, for not being paid nearly what you're worth, for taking the time to lend clarity to your words—which inspire as a result. I am honored to be in your company. Drinks in Maui on Karen.

To the women in my family: Mom and Lisa, who still make me laugh in my dreams; Anne, Julie, and Barbara, who provide endless inspiration.

To the men in my family: Dad and Rob, for their unquestioning support even when they wonder why I do these things.

To the good people at the *San Francisco Chronicle* (especially Phil), who both prodded me to take on the "Single Minded" column and then didn't hassle me when I was less productive than usual while I cranked this anthology out (especially David).

Acknowledgments

To my women friends who let me exploit their best stories in my column: Julia, Cynthia, Dayna, Tiffany, Kelly, Maya, Belle, Gayle, Michele, Vanessa, Ivory. You guys rock.

To all the men I've loved before: bygones, eh? I'll always have affection for you, since it's because of you that I get to be single.

And most especially to Erin, my daughter, who put up with all my zigs and zags and crying jags during my fitful journey into a fabulous, contented midlife. Darling one, I do this for you.

contributors

Kim Addonizio is the author of the novel *Little Beauties* (Simon & Schuster, 2005) and several acclaimed poetry collections, most recently *What Is This Thing Called Love.* Her previous collection, *Tell Me,* was a National Book Award finalist. She has also coauthored a book on writing poetry, *The Poet's Companion,* and coedited *Dorothy Parker's Elbow,* an anthology about tattoos. She lives in Oakland, California.

Isadora Alman is a California-licensed relationship therapist, a board-certified sexologist, the author of several books, and a syndicated sex and relationship columnist. Her "Ask Isadora" column has been running in alternative weekly papers worldwide for more than twenty years. Web surfers can find columns on her interactive Sexuality Forum at www.askisadora.com. She is a frequent TV and radio talk show guest, and a lecturer and workshop leader. She conducts her private counseling practice in San Francisco.

Judy Blunt spent more than thirty years on wheat and cattle ranches in northeastern Montana. Her poems and essays have appeared in numerous journals and anthologies, and she is the recipient of a 2005 National Endowment for the Arts fellowship. Her memoir,

Breaking Clean, was awarded a 1997 PEN/Jerard Fund Award for a work in progress, as well as a 2001 Whiting Writers' Award. She teaches nonfiction writing at the University of Montana, Missoula.

Anne Buelteman was raised in a Northern California airline-industry family so she comes by her wanderlust honestly. After more than a decade in the travel industry herself, she turned to her best love, the theater. Following a series of short-run shows, mostly musicals, she joined the national tour of a "Musical Sensation," and spent eleven years seeing North America and parts of Asia. She is living in Los Angeles, looking for the next job or ticket elsewhere. Meanwhile, she remains an intermittently zealous diarist who is considering writing a memoir. This is her first published work.

Liz Byrski is a writer and broadcaster who lives in Western Australia. She is the author of several nonfiction books; her first novel, *Gang of Four,* was published in 2004 by Macmillan. She lectures in professional writing at Curtin University, and her next novel, *Food, Sex and Money,* will be published in October 2005.

Ronnie Caplane, a resident of Piedmont, California, writes a biweekly column for two Knight Ridder–owned Bay Area newspapers. Her work has also appeared in various other publications, including the *Chicago Tribune, Cleveland Plain Dealer, Detroit Free Press, San Francisco Chronicle, San Francisco Examiner,* and the *Jewish Bulletin of Northern California* and other Jewish newspapers. A lawyer by trade, by day she is a commissioner on the California Workers' Compensation Appeals Board.

Dakota Cassidy writes erotic romance with a giggle. Her motto is: "Nothing in life can be right if you can't have a good laugh." Her Web site is www.dakotacassidy.com. She loves to hear from her readers!

Ellie Slott Fisher is the author of *Mom, There's a Man in the Kitchen and He's Wearing Your Robe: The Single Woman's Guide to Dating Well Without Parenting Poorly*. Fisher was a mother of two young children when her husband suddenly died, and she found herself returning to something she never imagined she would—dating. A former reporter and editor for United Press International, Fisher currently writes for magazines.

Laura Fraser is a San Francisco freelance writer and author, most recently of *An Italian Affair*, a best-selling travel memoir.

Lynn Freed is the author of seven books, most recently *Reading, Writing and Leaving Home*. Her work has appeared in *Harper's Magazine*, the *New Yorker*, the *Atlantic Monthly*, and the *New York Times*, among others, and has been widely translated. In 2002, she was awarded the inaugural Katherine Anne Porter Award by the American Academy of Arts and Letters. She has also received grants and fellowships from the National Endowment for the Arts and the Guggenheim Foundation. The *New York Times* named 2004's *The Curse of the Appropriate Man* a Notable Book of the Year. Having grown up in South Africa, she now lives in California.

Jane Ganahl has written for San Francisco daily newspapers for twenty years. Since early 2002, she has been writing the well-received "Single Minded"—a column by and for single women. Her work has also appeared on Salon.com and RollingStone.com and in various magazines, including *Book, Parenting*, and *Harp*. She has an essay in the anthology *Roar Softly and Carry a Great Lipstick* and is plotting her own memoir. She also organizes the Last Supper, a monthly dinner salon in San Francisco for creative people; codirects Litquake, an annual Bay Area literature festival; dates occasionally; and dotes on her twentysomething daughter. She is tired most of the time, but she really, *really* enjoys her unmarried life.

Spike Gillespie has been writing since she figured out how to hold a pencil. Her writing has appeared in the *New York Times Magazine, Smithsonian Magazine, National Geographic Traveler, Real Simple,* the *Washington Post, Playboy, GQ, Elle, Cosmo, Texas Monthly,* Salon.com, and *Nerve.* She is a former reporter and columnist for the *Dallas Morning News.* Gillespie's books include *All the Wrong Men and One Perfect Boy: A Memoir,* and most recently, *Surrender (But Don't Give Yourself Away): Old Cars, Found Hope, and Other Cheap Tricks,* an essay collection. She lives with twelve animals and her son Henry in Austin, Texas. Her Web site is www.spikeg.com.

Debra Ginsberg is the author of the critically acclaimed memoirs *Waiting, Raising Blaze,* and *About My Sisters.* She lives in Southern California.

Kathi Kamen Goldmark, founder of the all-author rock band Rock Bottom Remainders, is the author of *And My Shoes Keep Walking Back to You,* a novel; the coauthor of *The Great Rock & Roll Joke Book;* and a contributor to *My California: Journeys Made by Great Writers* and *Mid-life Confidential: The Rock Bottom Remainders Tour America with Three Chords and an Attitude.* She likes to think she is ready for anything. She lives in San Francisco.

Ms. Gonick writes the weekly column "Failing at Living" for the *San Francisco Chronicle.* In an earlier incarnation she wrote the monthly humor column "Mostly True Confessions" for *San Francisco Focus* magazine. She is a contributor to the anthology *Roar Softly and Carry a Great Lipstick* and the first grant recipient of the Anne and Robert Cowan Writers Fund. She lives and fails in the Bay Area.

Susan Griffin was named by *Utne Reader* as one of a hundred important visionaries for the new millennium and has been the recipient of a National Endowment for the Arts grant, a MacArthur Grant for Peace and International Cooperation, and an Emmy Award (for her play, *Voices*). Among her books are *The Book of the Courtesans: A Catalogue of Their Virtues, Woman and Nature, What Her Body Thought,* and *A Chorus of Stones* (finalist for both the Pulitzer Prize and the National Book Critics Circle Award and winner of the BABRA award in 1992). Her recent essays on gender and society were collected in *The Eros of Everyday Life.* She has also published several volumes of award-winning poetry (*Unremembered Country, Bending Home,* and *Selected and New Poems*). She teaches privately in Berkeley, where she lives not far from her daughter and her grandchildren.

Sam Horn, twelve-time emcee of the Maui Writers Conference, president of Action Keynotes-Creative-Consulting, and author of *Tongue Fu!, What's Holding You Back, ConZentrate,* and *Take the Bully by the Horns,* helps people get their books out of their head and into the world. For more information about her programs and products, visit www.SamHorn.com or call 800-SAM-3455.

Jane Juska was born seventy-two years ago in Ann Arbor, Michigan. Retired from thirty-three years of teaching English in high school, college, and prison, she took up writing full time and seriously. In her sixty-sixth year, she placed an ad in the *New York Review of Books*: "Before I turn 67 I would like to have a lot of sex with a man I like." Her book, *A Round-Heeled Woman: My Late-Life Adventures in Sex and Romance,* showed what happened then—a lot. Her next book, *Unaccompanied Women,* will show what happened after *that*—a lot. It will appear in 2006.

Patti Lawson is the author of *The Dog Diet: Lighten Up Your Life and Your Body Will Follow.* She writes a column for the *Charleston Gazette* titled "Dogs . . . Diets . . . Dating." She lives in West Virginia with Sadie, her canine soul mate; practices law; and is in demand as a public speaker. Her Web site can be found at www.thedogdiet.com.

Diane Mapes has written humorous essays on pop culture, the single life, television, travel, naked sushi, and more for *Bust*, *Health*, the *Los Angeles Times*, *Mental Floss*, *Seattle Magazine*, the *Washington Post*, and other publications. A native and resident of the Pacific Northwest, she grew up on a strawberry farm with four sisters and one overworked mother. She is happily single.

Five-time Emmy Award–winning writer **Merrill Markoe** has published three books of humorous essays and the novels *The Psycho Ex Game* (with Andy Prieboy) and *It's My F—ing Birthday*. She has worked as a radio host and a TV correspondent and has written for television, movies, and an assortment of publications.

Susan Maushart is a columnist for the *Weekend Australia* magazine and a senior research fellow in the Division of Humanities at Curtin University of Technology in Western Australia. In 2004 she released *Wifework: What Marriage Really Means for Women*; her latest book, *What Women Want Next*, is about feminism and happiness.

Joyce Maynard has been a reporter and columnist for the *New York Times*, a frequent commentator on NPR, and a longtime magazine journalist as well as a teacher of writing. Author of the memoir *At Home in the World*, she is also the author of five novels, including *To Die For* and (most recently) *The Cloud Chamber* (Simon and Schuster, 2005). The mother of three grown children, she makes her home in Mill Valley, California, and Lake Atitlan, Guatemala. Her Web site is www.JoyceMaynard.com.

Wendy Merrill has been conducting undercover operations in the arena of dating for many years, earning her several advanced degrees. Her unique "catch and release" program has provided a rich body of data, and she's currently in California compiling her research for a collection entitled *Falling into Manholes*.

Irene Sherlock's poems and essays have been published in

Amaranth, Calyx, Cream City Review, Connecticut Review, poem-memoir-story, Poetry Motel, Roux, Runes, Slipstream, the *New York Times,* and several anthologies. Her essays can be heard on WSHU National Public Radio.

April Sinclair is the author of three novels: the critically acclaimed best-seller *Coffee Will Make You Black, Ain't Gonna Be the Same Fool Twice,* and *I Left My Back Door Open.* Sinclair received the Carl Sandburg Award from the Friends of the Chicago Public Library for *Coffee Will Make You Black,* which the American Library Association named a Book of the Year in 1994 (Young Adult Fiction). Sinclair has been a fellow at the Ragdale, MacDowell, Yaddo, and Djerassi artist colonies. She lives in Berkeley and is working on her fourth novel.

Sunny Singh was born in Varanasi, India. She published her first novel, *Nani's Book of Suicides,* in 2000. In 2003, the novel's translation in Spanish was awarded the Novela de la Diversidad award at the Mar de Letras festival in Cartagena, Spain. Her second book, *Single in the City: The Independent Woman's Handbook,* was declared "an empowering read." Her third book, and second novel, *With Krishna's Eyes,* is due for publication later in 2005. Singh has worked as a teacher, a journalist, and an executive for multinationals in Chile, South Africa, and Mexico. She also writes for the theater. She lives in Barcelona, Spain.

Rachel Toor is the author of *The Pig and I: How I Learned to Love Men as Much as I Love My Pets.* She has been the adoring companion of a mouse, a rat, a dog, a cat, a horse, an ass, and a pig. She received her BA from Yale and spent a dozen years as an editor of scholarly books, after which she became an admissions counselor at Duke University. She is also the author of *Admissions Confidential: An Insider's Account of the Elite College Selection Process.* She lives—with neither man nor animal—in Missoula, Montana.

Cameron Tuttle is the author of the best-selling *Bad Girl's Guides* (Chronicle Books) and cocreator of the television sitcom based on her books. She founded and launched Badgirlswirl.com, an online community and store, which was nominated for a 2003 Webby Award. The *Bad Girl's Guide* franchise, which continues to grow with new products, has sold well over a million copies. In the March 2003 issue of *Fast Company*, Tuttle was named one of the Fast 50, honored as an innovator in the business of culture. She has a degree in English poetry from Brown University and lives in San Francisco with her fears and a sense of humor. To reach her, please visit www.badgirlswirl.com.

COPYRIGHT NOTICES